The

Swimming Strokes

Book

82 Easy Exercises
For Learning How To Swim
The Four Basic Swimming Strokes

Mark Young

Author Online!

For more resources and swimming help visit
Mark Young's website at

www.swim-teach.com

Mark Young is a well-established swimming instructor with over twenty years experience of teaching thousands of adults and children to swim. He has taken nervous, frightened children and adults with a fear of water and made them happy and confident swimmers.   He has also turned many of average ability into advanced swimmers. This book draws on his experiences and countless successes to put together this simplistic methodical approach to swimming.

Also by Mark Young

How To Be A Swimming Teacher
The Definitive Guide to Becoming a
Successful Swimming Teacher

The Complete Guide To Simple Swimming
Everything You Need to Know from Your First Entry into the Pool to Swimming the Four Basic Strokes

A Catalogue record for this book is available from the British Library

ISBN 9780992742829

Published by: Educate & Learn Publishing, Hertfordshire, UK

Graphics by Mark Young, courtesy of Poser V6.0

Design and typeset by Mark Young

Published in association with www.swim-teach.com

Contents

Page

How to use this book

Learning how to swim can be a frustrating experience sometimes, especially for an adult. Kick with your legs, pull with your arms, breathe in, and breathe out and do it all at the right time. Before you know it you've got a hundred and one things to think about and do all at the same time or in the right sequence.

The Swimming Strokes Book is designed to break each stroke down into its component parts, those parts being body position, legs, arms, breathing and timing and coordination. An exercise or series of exercises are then assigned to that part along with relevant teaching points and technique tips, to help focus only on that stroke part.

The 82 exercises form reference sections for each swimming stroke, complete with technique tips, teaching points and common mistakes for each individual exercise.

What exactly are these exercises?

Each specific exercise focuses on a certain part of the swimming stroke, for example the body position, the leg kick, the arms, the breathing or the timing and coordination, all separated into easy to learn stages. Each one contains a photograph of the exercise being performed, a graphical diagram and all the technique elements and key focus points that are relevant to that particular exercise.

How will they help?

They break down your swimming technique into its core elements and then force you to focus on that certain area. For example if you are performing a leg kick exercise, the leg kick is isolated and therefore your focus and concentration is only on the legs. The technical information and key focus points then fix your concentration on the most important elements of the leg kick. The result: a more efficient and technically correct leg kick. The same then goes for exercises for the arms, breathing, timing and coordination and so on.

Will they help to learn and improve your swimming strokes?

Yes, definitely! Although it is not the same as having a swimming teacher with you to correct you, these practical exercises perfectly compliment lessons or help to enhance your practice time in the pool. They not only isolate certain areas but also can highlight your bad habits. Once you've worked though each element of the stroke and practiced the exercises a few times, you will slowly eliminate your bad habits. The result: a more efficient and technically correct swimming stroke, swum with less effort!

Front Crawl

technique overview

Swimming with good front crawl technique is a desire that many long for. Whether its for competition, triathlon or just to feel and look good in your local pool, front crawl is the swimming stroke everyone wants to know how to swim well.

Front crawl is the fastest, most efficient stroke of them all. This is largely down to the streamlined body position and continuous propulsion from the arms and legs. The alternating action of the arms and legs is relatively easy on the joints and the stroke as a whole develops aerobic capacity faster than any other stroke. In competitive terms it is usually referred to as Freestyle.

The constant alternating arm action generates almost all of the propulsion and is the most efficient arm action of the four basic swimming strokes. The leg action promotes a horizontal, streamlined body position and balances the arm action but provides little propulsion.

Front crawl breathing technique requires the head to be turned so that the mouth clears the water but causes minimal upset to the balance of the body from its normal streamlined position.

The timing and coordination of the arms and legs occur most commonly with six leg kicks to one arm cycle. However, stroke timing can vary, with a four beat cycle and even a two beat cycle, which is most commonly used in long distance swims and endurance events.

Body Position

The overall body position for front crawl is as streamlined and as flat as possible at the water surface, with the head in-line with the body.

The waterline is around the natural hairline with eyes looking forward and down.

If the position of the head is raised it will cause the position of the hips and legs to lower which in turn will increase frontal resistance, causing the stroke to be inefficient and the breathing technique to be incorrect.

If the head position is too low it will cause the legs to rise and the kick to lose its efficiency.

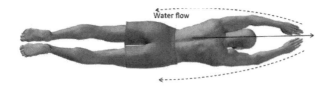

Streamlined body position minimises drag, allowing efficient movement through the water

Shoulders remain at the surface and roll with the arm action. Hips also roll with the stroke technique, close to the water surface and the legs remain in line with the body.

Common Body Position Mistakes

The common body position mistakes made are with head position and hand and feet position during the stroke.

If the head is too high over the water surface, it will cause the legs and feet to be lower under the water surface and cause the overall body position to be angled and therefore very inefficient.

Hands and feet must be together throughout the swimming stroke as this gives the body its streamlined efficiency, allowing it to move smoothly though the water.

If the hands or feet move apart it causes the overall shape of the body in the water to become wider and therefore inefficient.

The best exercise to practice perfecting the correct body position and shape is a push and glide from the poolside. The swimmer pushes off from the pool wall or floor and glides across the water surface, keeping the head central and hands and feet touching together.

Leg Kick

The leg kick for front crawl originates from the hips and both legs kick with equal force.

The legs kick in an up and down alternating action, with the propulsive phase coming from the down kick. There should be a slight bend in the knee due to the water pressure, in order to produce the propulsion required on the down kick.

Toes are pointed to provide streamline effect and ankles are relaxed

Downward kick provides propulsion   Knee is relaxed and slightly bent

The downward kick begins at the hip and uses the thigh muscles to straighten the leg at the knee, ending with the foot extended to allow it's surface area to bear upon the water. As the leg moves upwards, the sole of the foot and the back of the leg press upwards and backwards against the water.

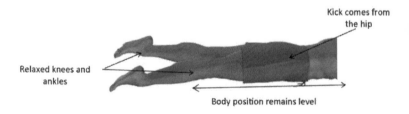

Kick comes from the hip

Relaxed knees and ankles

Body position remains level

13

The upward kick slows and stops as the leg nears and minimally breaks the water surface. Ankles are relaxed and toes pointed to give an in-toeing effect when kicking and the leg kick depth should be within the overall depth of the body.

Common Leg Kick Mistakes

It is very common to kick from the knees during front crawl, in an attempt to generate some propulsion and movement. This can also lead to a very stiff and robotic kicking action. The kick must originate from the hip and be a smooth movement with relaxed knee and ankle joints.

Another common mistake is to make the kicking movements too large. In other words, the feet come out over the water surface causing excessive splash and again wasting valuable energy.

A good exercise to practice the leg kick is holding a float or a kick board and kicking along the length of the pool with face down. This will allow the swimmer to focus purely on the leg kick, ensuring it is a relaxed and flowing up and down movement.

The continuous alternating arm action provides the majority of the power and propulsion of the entire swimming stroke.

entry

The hand enters the water at a 45 degree angle, finger tips first, thumb side down. The hand entry should be between shoulder and head line with a slight elbow bend.

catch

The hand reaches forward under the water without over stretching and the arm fully extends just under the water surface.

propulsive phase

The hand sweeps through the water downwards, inwards and then upwards. The elbow is high at the end of the down sweep and remains high throughout the in-sweep. The hand pulls through towards the thigh and upwards to the water surface.

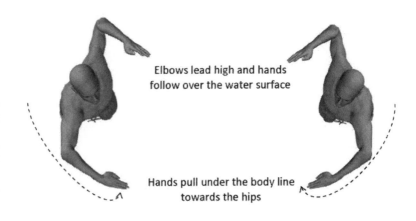

Elbows lead high and hands follow over the water surface

Hands pull under the body line towards the hips

recovery phase

The elbow bends to exit the water first. Hand and fingers fully exit the water and follow a straight path along the bodyline over the water surface. The elbow is bent and high and the arm is fully relaxed.

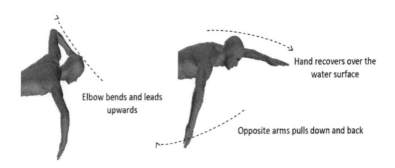

Elbow bends and leads upwards

Hand recovers over the water surface

Opposite arms pulls down and back

Common Arm Technique Mistakes

The arm action can bring about many mistakes, the most common being a deep propulsive phase and a very high recovery phase.

Both of these mistakes will disturb the body position, which will in turn create an inefficient overall swimming stroke. Both a deep arm pull and a high arm recovery over the water surface will also cause excessive body roll.

The best exercise for practicing and correcting these common mistakes is holding a float in one hand and swimming using single arm pulls. This will force the swimmer to focus on the arm technique whilst ensuring that the body position remains level and correct.

The head turns to the side on inhalation for front crawl breathing technique. The head begins to turn at the end of the upward arm sweep and turns enough for the mouth to clear the water and inhale. The head turns back into the water just as the arm recovers over and the hand returns to the water. Breathing can be bilateral (alternate sides every one and a half stroke cycles) or unilateral (same side) depending of the stroke cycle and distance to be swum.

Breath IN as the arm pulls through and the head turns to the side

Types of Breathing Technique

Trickle Breathing

The breath is slowly exhaled through the mouth and nose into the water during the propulsive phase of the arm pull. The exhalation is controlled to allow inhalation to take place easily as the arm recovers.

Explosive Breathing

The breath is held after inhalation during the propulsive arm
phase and then released explosively, part in and part out of the
water, as the head is turned to the side.

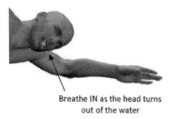

Breathe IN as the head turns
out of the water

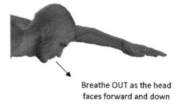

Breathe OUT as the head
faces forward and down

Common Breathing Mistakes

It is very common, especially for beginners, to perform explosive
breathing without knowing they are doing so. Holding the breath
during the swimming stroke comes naturally to most people but
it is not necessarily the most energy efficient way of swimming.

Breath holding causes an increase in carbon dioxide in the
system, which increase the urgency to breathe. This can cause
swimmers to become breathless very quickly.

Trickle breathing is the most effective breathing technique for
beginners as it allows a gentle release of carbon dioxide from the
lungs, which then makes inhalation easier.

Another common mistake is to lift the head instead of roll the
head to the side. Lifting the head causes the legs to sink and the

overall body position to be disturbed and the swimming stroke to be inefficient.

The best exercise for perfecting trickle breathing and ensuring the head is not lifting is to hold a float with a diagonal grip and kick. The diagonal grip allows space for the head to roll to the side.

Timing

The timing and coordination for front crawl usually occurs naturally.

The arms should provide a powerful propulsive alternating action whilst leg kicks also remain continuous and alternating.

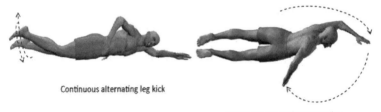

Continuous alternating leg kick

Continuous alternating arm action

However, there are a few variations.

Six beat cycle – each leg kicks three down kicks per arm cycle. The cycle is normally taught to beginners and used for sprint swims. Four beat cycle – each leg kicks down twice for each arm pull. Two-beat cycle – each leg kicks one downbeat per arm cycle. Long distance swimmers normally use this timing cycle, where the leg kick acts as a counter balance instead of a source of propulsion.

Common Mistakes

These various timing and coordination cycles bring varying degrees of mistakes, the most common being an attempt to kick too fast.

The required speed of the leg kick and therefore the timing cycle required for the stroke depends on the distance that is to be swum. A long distance swim requires the leg kick to counter balance the arm action, so the two beat cycle is best used. The short sprint requires a faster leg kick so the six beat cycle is needed so that the legs can provide more propulsion.

It is easy to kick with a fast leg kick and unknowingly allow the arm action to also speed up. This results in a loss of arm technique and overall body shape leading to a poor and inefficient swimming stroke.

Catch up is the best swimming exercise to not only establish correct timing and coordination cycle but to experiment with different timing cycles, as the delayed arm action slows down the exercise.

Front Crawl

exercises

FRONT CRAWL: Body Position

Holding the poolside

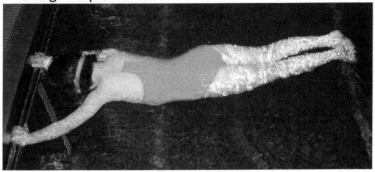

Aim: to encourage confidence in a floating position.

The swimmer holds the poolside for added security and some assistance may be required, as some people will not naturally float.

Hands holding the
poolside or rail

Overall body position is as horizontal as possible,
depending on the swimmers own buoyancy.

Key Actions

Relax
Keep the head tucked between the arms
Stretch out as far as you can
Keep your feet together

Technical Focus

Head is central and still
Face is submerged
Eyes are looking downwards
Shoulders should be level
Hips are close to the surface
Legs are together and in line with the body

Common Faults

Failure to submerge the face
Overall body is not relaxed
Head is not central
Whole body is not remaining straight
Feet are not together

FRONT CRAWL: Body Position

Static practice holding floats

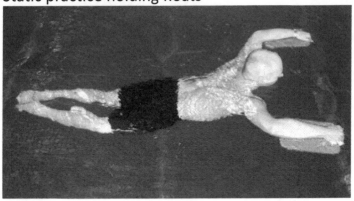

Aim: to help the swimmer develop confidence in their own buoyancy.

A float can be held under each arm or a single float held out in front, depending on levels of confidence and ability. Some swimmers may need extra assistance if they lack natural buoyancy.

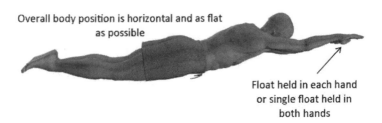

Overall body position is horizontal and as flat as possible

Float held in each hand or single float held in both hands

Key Actions
Relax
Keep the head tucked between the arms
Stretch out as far as you can
Keep your feet together

Technical Focus
Head is central and still
Face is submerged
Eyes are looking downwards
Shoulders should be level
Hips are close to the surface
Legs are together and in line with the body

Common Faults
Failure to submerge the face
Head is not central
Whole body is not remaining straight
Feet and hands are not together

FRONT CRAWL: Body Position

Push and glide from standing

 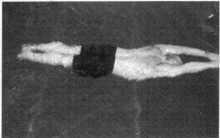

Aim: to develop correct body position and confidence in pushing off.

The swimmer can start with arms stretched out in front and pushes off from the pool floor or from the wall with one foot and glides through the water unaided.

Legs push off from
pool side or pool floor

Direction of travel

Key Actions
Push hard from the side/pool floor
Keep your head tucked between your arms
Stretch out as far as you can
Keep your hands together
Keep your feet together

Technical Focus
Initial push should be enough to gain good movement
Head remains still and central
Face submerged so that the water is at brow level
Shoulders should be level
Legs in line with the body

Common Faults
Failure to submerge the face
Push off is too weak
Whole body is not remaining straight
Feet are not together

FRONT CRAWL: Body Position

Push and glide from the side holding floats

Aim: to develop correct body position whilst moving through the water.

Body position should be laying prone with the head up at this stage. The use of floats helps to build confidence, particularly in the weak or nervous swimmer. The floats create a slight resistance to the glide, but this is still a useful exercise.

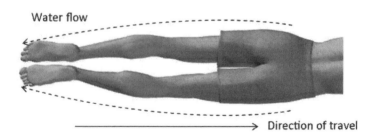

Water flow

Direction of travel

Key Actions
Push hard from the wall
Relax and float across the water
Keep your head still and look forward
Stretch out as far as you can
Keep your feet together

Technical Focus
Head remains still and central with the chin on the water surface
Eyes are looking forwards and downwards
Shoulders should be level and square
Hips are close to the surface
Legs are in line with the body

Common Faults
Push from the side is not hard enough
Head is not central
Whole body is not remaining straight
Feet are not together

FRONT CRAWL: Body Position

Push and glide from the poolside

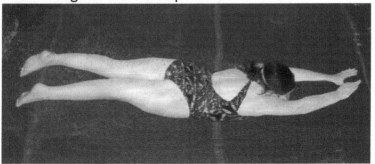

Aim: to develop a streamlined body position whilst moving thorough the water.

Movement is created by pushing and gliding from holding position at the poolside.

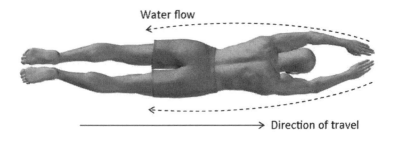

Water flow

Direction of travel

Streamlined body position minimises drag, allowing efficient movement through the water

Technical Focus
Head remains still and central
Face submerged so that the water is at brow level
Shoulders should be level and square
Legs are in line with the body
Overall body position should be streamlined

Key Actions
Push hard from the side
Stretch your arms out in front as you push
Keep your head tucked between your arms
Stretch out as far as you can
Keep your hands and feet together

Common Faults
Push off is too weak
Arms stretch in front after the push
Head is not central
Overall body position not in line
Hands or feet are not together

FRONT CRAWL: Legs

Sitting on the poolside kicking

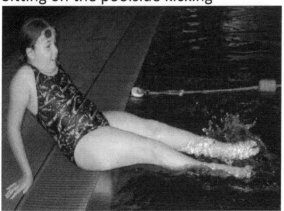

Aim: to give the swimmer the feel of the water during the kick.

Sitting on poolside kicking is an ideal exercise for the beginner to practise correct leg kicking action with the added confidence of sitting on the poolside.

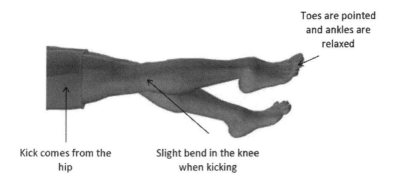

Toes are pointed and ankles are relaxed

Kick comes from the hip

Slight bend in the knee when kicking

Key Actions
Kick with straight legs
Pointed toes
Make a small splash with your toes
Kick with floppy feet
Kick continuously

Technical Focus
Kick is continuous and alternating
Knee is only slightly bent
Legs are close together when they kick
Ankles are relaxed and the toes are pointed

Common Faults
Knees bend too much
Kick comes from the knee
Stiff ankles

FRONT CRAWL: Legs

Holding the poolside

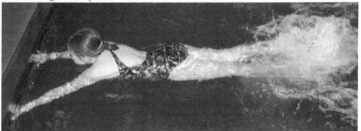

Aim: to encourage the swimmer to learn the kicking action.

Holding the poolside enhances confidence and helps develop leg strength and technique.

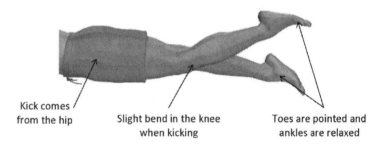

Kick comes from the hip

Slight bend in the knee when kicking

Toes are pointed and ankles are relaxed

Key Actions
Kick with straight legs
Pointed toes
Make a small splash with your toes
Kick with floppy feet
Kick from your hips
Kick continuously
Legs kick close together

Technical Focus
Kick comes from the hip
Kick is continuous and alternating
Knee is only slightly bent
Legs are close together when they kick
Ankles are relaxed and the toes are pointed
Kick should just break the water surface

Common Faults
Feet come out of the water
Kick comes from the knee
Legs are too deep in the water

FRONT CRAWL: Legs

Legs kick with a float held under each arm

Aim: to learn correct kicking technique and develop leg strength.

The added stability of two floats will help boost confidence in the weak swimmer.

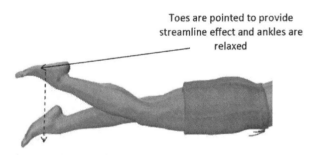

Toes are pointed to provide streamline effect and ankles are relaxed

Downward kick provides propulsion

Key Actions
Kick with straight legs
Pointed toes
Kick with floppy feet
Kick from your hips
Kick continuously

Technical Focus
Kick comes from the hip
Kick is continuous and alternating
Chin remains on the water surface
Legs are close together when they kick
Ankles are relaxed and the toes are pointed
Kick should just break the water surface
Upper body and arms should be relaxed

Common Faults
Head lifts above the surface, causing the legs to sink
Kick comes from the knee causing excessive bend
Kick is not deep enough
Legs are too deep in the water

FRONT CRAWL: Legs

Float held with both hands

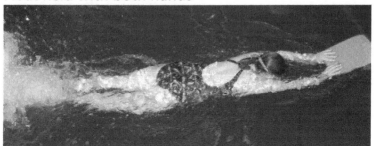

Aim: to practise and learn correct kicking technique.

Holding a float or kickboard out in front isolates the legs, encourages correct body position and develops leg strength.

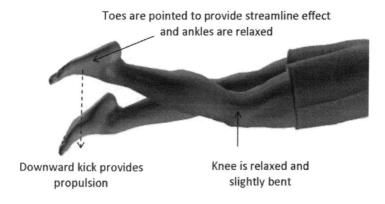

Toes are pointed to provide streamline effect and ankles are relaxed

Downward kick provides propulsion

Knee is relaxed and slightly bent

Key Actions
Kick with pointed toes
Make a small splash with your toes
Kick with floppy feet
Legs kick close together

Technical Focus
Kick comes from the hip
Kick is continuous and alternating.
Legs are close together when they kick
Ankles are relaxed and the toes are pointed.
Kick should just break the water surface.

Common Faults
Knees bend too much
Feet come out of the water
Kick comes from the knee
Legs are too deep in the water

FRONT CRAWL: Legs

Push and glide with added leg kick

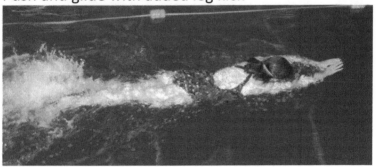

Aim: to develop correct body position and leg kick whilst holding the breath.

Push and glide without a float and add a leg kick whilst maintaining a streamlined body position.

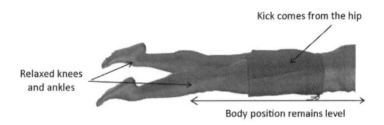

Kick comes from the hip

Relaxed knees and ankles

Body position remains level

Key Actions
Kick with straight legs and pointed toes
Kick with floppy feet
Kick from your hips
Kick continuously

Technical Focus
Kick comes from the hip
Streamlined body position is maintained
Kick is continuous and alternating
Legs are close together when they kick
Ankles are relaxed and the toes are pointed
Kick should just break the water surface

Common Faults
Feet come out of the water
Stiff ankles
Kick is not deep enough
Legs are too deep in the water

FRONT CRAWL: Legs

Leg kick whilst holding a float vertically in front

Aim: to create resistance and help develop strength and stamina.

Holding a float vertically in front increases the intensity of the kicking action, which in turn develops leg strength and stamina.

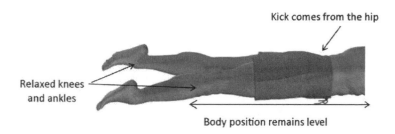

Kick comes from the hip

Relaxed knees and ankles

Body position remains level

Key Actions
Kick with straight legs and pointed toes
Kick with floppy feet
Kick from your hips
Kick continuously

Technical Focus
Kick comes from the hip
Streamlined body position is maintained
Kick is continuous and alternating
Legs are close together when they kick
Ankles are relaxed and the toes are pointed
Kick should just break the water surface

Common Faults
Feet come out of the water
Stiff ankles
Kick is not deep enough
Legs are too deep in the water

FRONT CRAWL: Arms

Standing on the poolside or in shallow water

Aim: to practise correct arm movement whilst in a static position.

This is an exercise for beginners that can be practised on the poolside or standing in shallow water.

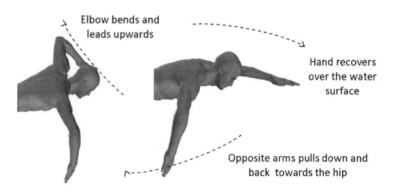

Elbow bends and leads upwards

Hand recovers over the water surface

Opposite arms pulls down and back towards the hip

Key Actions
Keep your fingers together
Continuous smooth action
Brush your hand past your thigh
Gradually bend your elbow

Technical Focus
Fingers should be together
Pull through to the hips
Elbow bends and leads upwards

Common Faults
Fingers are too wide apart
Pull is short and not to the thigh
Arms are too straight as they pull
Arms are too straight on recovery
Hand entry is wide of the shoulder line

FRONT CRAWL: Arms

Single arm practice with float held in one hand

Aim: to practise and improve correct arm technique

This practice allows the swimmer to develop arm technique whilst maintaining body position and leg kick. Holding a float with one hand gives the weaker swimmer security and allows the competent swimmer to focus on a single arm.

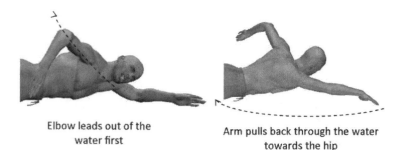

Elbow leads out of the water first

Arm pulls back through the water towards the hip

Key Actions

Keep your fingers together
Brush your hand past your thigh
Pull fast under the water
Make an 'S' shape under the water
Elbow out first
Reach over the water surface

Technical Focus

Fingertips enter first with thumb side down
Fingers should be together
Pull should be an elongated 'S' shape
Pull through to the hips
Elbow exits the water first
Fingers clear the water on recovery

Common Faults

Fingers are apart
Pull is short and not to the thigh
Lack of power in the pull
Arm pull is too deep underwater
Arms are too straight on recovery

FRONT CRAWL: Arms

Alternating arm pull whilst holding a float out in front

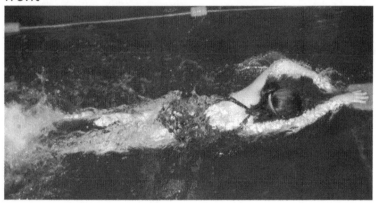

Aim: to develop coordination and correct arm pull technique.

The swimmer uses an alternating arm action. This also introduces a timing aspect, as the leg kick has to be continuous at the same time.

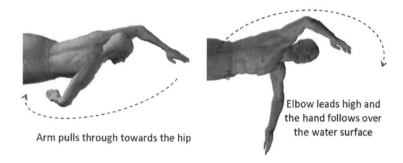

Arm pulls through towards the hip

Elbow leads high and the hand follows over the water surface

Key Actions
Finger tips in first
Brush your hand past your thigh
Pull fast under the water
Elbow out first
Reach over the water surface

Technical Focus
Clean entry with fingertips first and thumb side down
Fingers should be together
Each arm pulls through to the hips
Elbow leads out first
Fingers clear the water on recovery

Common Faults
Fingers are too wide apart
Pull is short and not to the thigh
Lack of power in the pull
Arms are too straight on recovery
Hand entry is wide of shoulder line

FRONT CRAWL: Arms

Arm action using a pull-buoy

Aim: to develop arm pull strength, technique and coordination.

This is a more advanced exercise, which requires stamina and a degree of breathing technique.

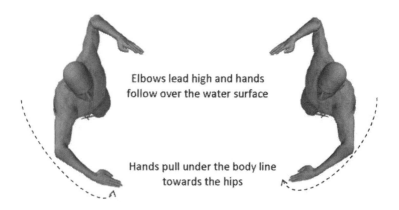

Elbows lead high and hands follow over the water surface

Hands pull under the body line towards the hips

Key Actions
Long strokes
Smooth continuous action
Brush your hand past your thigh
Make an 'S' shape under the water
Elbow out first
Reach over the water surface

Technical Focus
Fingertips enter first with thumb side down
Fingers should be together
Pull should be an elongated 'S' shape
Pull through to the hips
Elbow comes out first
Fingers clear the water on recovery

Common Faults
Pull is short and not to the thigh
Lack of power in the pull
Arms pull too deep under water
Arms are too straight on recovery
Hand entry is across the centre line

FRONT CRAWL: Arms

Push and glide adding arm cycles

Aim: to combine correct arm action with a streamlined body position.

The swimmer performs a push and glide to establish body position and then adds arm cycles, whilst maintaining body position.

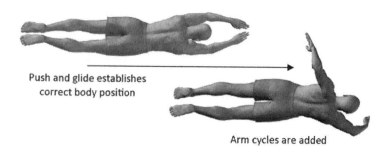

Push and glide establishes correct body position

Arm cycles are added

Key Actions

Finger tips in the water first
Brush your hand past your thigh
Make an 'S' shape under the water
Elbow out first
Reach over the water surface

Technical Focus

Clean entry with fingertips first
Pull should be an elongated 'S' shape
Pull through to the hips
Elbow comes out first
Fingers clear the water on recovery

Common Faults

Pull is short and not to the thigh
Lack of power in the pull
Arms are too straight under water
Arms are too straight on recovery
Hand entry is across centre line

FRONT CRAWL: Breathing
Standing and holding the poolside

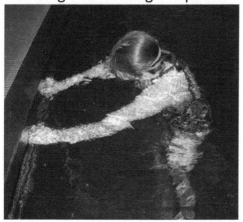

Aim: to practice and develop breathing technique.
The pupil stands and holds the pool rail with one arm extended, breathing to one side to introduce the beginner to breathing whilst having his/her face submerged.

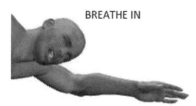

BREATHE IN

Head turns to the side and mouth clears the water surface

BREATHE OUT

Head faces forward and down

Key Actions
Breathe out through your mouth
Blow out slowly and gently
Turn your head to the side when you breathe in
See how long you can make the breath last

Technical Focus
Breathing should be from the mouth
Breathing in should be when the head is turned to the side
Breathing out should be when the face is down

Common Faults
Breathing through the nose
Holding the breath

FRONT CRAWL: Breathing

Holding a float in front with diagonal grip

Aim: to encourage correct breathing technique whilst kicking.

The float is held in front; one arm extended fully, the other holding the near corner with elbow low. This creates a gap for the head and mouth to be turned in at the point of breathing.

Breathe IN as the head turns out of the water

Breathe OUT as the head faces forward and down

Key Actions
Turn head towards the bent arm to breathe
Breathe out through your mouth
Blow out slowly and gently
Return head to the centre soon after breathing

Technical Focus
Breathing should be from the mouth
Breathing in should be when the head is turned to the side
Breathing out should be slow and controlled

Common Faults
Breathing through the nose
Holding the breath
Lifting the head and looking forward when breathing
Turning towards the straight arm

FRONT CRAWL: Breathing

Float held in one hand, arm action with breathing

Aim: to develop correct breathing technique whilst pulling with one arm.

This allows the swimmer to add the arm action to the breathing technique and perfect the timing of the two movements. The float provides support and keeps the exercise as a simple single arm practice.

Breath IN as the arm pulls through and the head turns to the side

Key Actions

Turn head to the side of the pulling arm
Breathe out through your mouth
Blow out slowly and gently
Return head to the centre soon after breathing

Technical Focus

Head moves enough for mouth to clear the water
Breathing in occurs when the head is turned to the side
Breathing out should be slow
Breathing should be from the mouth

Common Faults

Turning towards the straight arm
Turning the head too much
Breathing through the nose
Holding the breath
Lifting the head and looking forward when breathing

FRONT CRAWL: Breathing

Float held in both hands, alternate arm pull with breathing

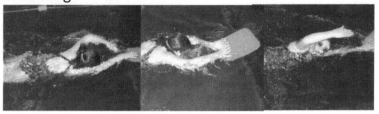

Aim: to practise bi-lateral breathing with the support of a float held out in front.

A single float is held in both hands and one arm pull is performed at a time with the head turning to breathe with each arm pull. Different arm action and breathing cycles can be used, for example; breathe every other arm pull or every three arm pulls.

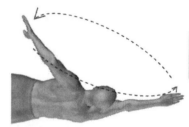

Head turns to the left side as the left arm pulls through and begins to recover

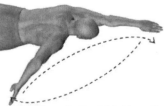

Head turns to the right side as the right arm pulls through and begins to recover

Key Actions

Keep head still until you need to breathe
Breathe every 3 strokes (or another pattern you may choose)
Turn head to the side as your arm pulls back
Return head to the centre soon after breathing
Breathe out through your mouth

Technical Focus

Head should be still when not taking a breath
Head movement should be minimal enough for mouth to clear
the water
Breathing in should be when the head is turned to the side
Breathing should be from the mouth

Common Faults

Turning towards the straight arm
Turning the head too much
Turning the head too early or late to breath
Lifting the head and looking forward when breathing

FRONT CRAWL: Timing

Front crawl catch up

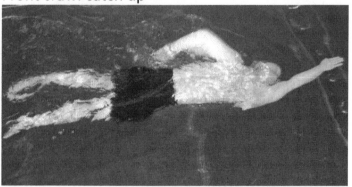

Aim: to practice correct stroke timing and develop coordination.

The opposite arm remains stationary until the arm performing the pull recovers to its starting position. This is an advanced exercise and encourages the swimmer to maintain body position and leg kick whilst practicing arm cycles.

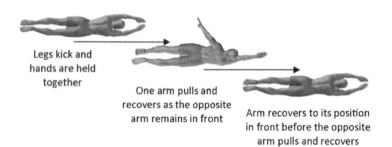

Legs kick and hands are held together

One arm pulls and recovers as the opposite arm remains in front

Arm recovers to its position in front before the opposite arm pulls and recovers

Key Actions
Finger tips in the water first
Brush your hand past your thigh
Make an 'S' shape under the water
Elbow out first
Reach over the water surface

Technical Focus
Clean entry with fingertips first
Pull should be an elongated 'S' shape
Pull through to the hips
Elbow comes out first
Fingers clear the water on recovery

Common Faults
One leg kick per arm pull ('one beat cycle')
Continuous leg kick but not enough arm pulls
Arm pull is too irregular

FRONT CRAWL
Full stroke

Aim: full stroke Front Crawl demonstrating correct leg action, arm action, breathing and timing.

Key Actions
Keep your head still until you breathe
Kick continuously from your hips
Stretch forward with each arm action
Pull continuously under your body
Count 3 leg kicks with each arm pull

Technical Focus
Stroke is smooth and continuous
Head in line with the body
Legs in line with the body
Head remains still
Leg kick is continuous and alternating
Arm action is continuous and alternating
Breathing is regular and to the side
Stroke ideally has a 6 beat cycle

Common Faults
Head moves from side to side
Legs kick from the knee
Leg action is too slow
Arm action is untidy and splashing
Excessive head movement when breathing o Head is lifted, causing legs to sink
Stroke is erratic and rushed

Front Crawl

common questions

When I swim front crawl I have to hold my breath, because my head does not come out of the water enough for me to catch any air. What am I doing wrong?

Firstly the fact that you are holding your breath in the first place can sometimes cause problems. If you hold your breath you have only a split second to breathe out and then in again, which can be very difficult. So much so that pupils I have taught in the past turn their head as if to breathe but continue to hold their breath.

It could be that your mouth is clearing the water enough to breathe but you are involuntarily continuing to hold your breath.

To overcome this you must breathe out into the water whilst swimming and then when you turn your head to breathe, you only have to breathe in. This makes breathing easier and more relaxed.

If as you suspect the problem is your head not clearing the water surface enough then we need to look at the basics of the breathing technique.

Firstly front crawl breathing technique involves rolling the head to one side and not lifting the head to face forward. Lifting your head upwards will result in that sinking feeling and your mouth will almost certainly not clear the water enough to breathe in.

Ensure that at the point where you roll your head to the side to breathe, your arm on that side must have pulled back to clear a space for your head to turn into. You must then breathe in just as your arm recovers over the water surface.

To ensure that your head rolls to the side enough try looking at your shoulder as you do it. This will ensure you are actually rolling your head and not lifting it. It will also help your mouth to
68

clear to water so that you can breathe.

If you are still struggling try to exaggerate your movement by rolling your head to look at ceiling above you. Your arm recovery will have to be very high in order to achieve this but it will almost certainly allow you to breathe. However, this is of course technically incorrect but the exaggerated movement will allow you to practice the movement and become confident with breathing. It is therefore important to readjust the technique once you have become proficient by rolling the head the minimum amount so as not to disturb your overall body position.

How do I coordinate the arms and legs for front crawl? I am just learning to swim and when swimming my arms my legs will not move in time with each other.

The problem you are referring to is related to your coordination.

Front crawl is an alternating stroke. In other words as one arm pulls the other recovers and as one leg kicks downwards the other kicks upwards.

Unlike breaststroke which is a simultaneous swimming stroke where both arms pull at the same time and both legs also kick at the same time.

You will find that your coordination will favour one more than the other because one will come more naturally than the other.

The timing and coordination of front crawl arms and legs is not something that comes naturally to some people but there is no reason why it cannot be learnt.

A simple exercise to try out is front crawl 'catch up'. Hold a float or kick board with both hands and kick your legs. Then perform one arm pull at a time, taking hold of the float after each complete arm action. You are therefore performing front crawl arms one at a time whilst attempting to maintain your leg kick. Holding the float will help you to focus on your leg kick whilst using your arms.

As for how fast to kick your legs, there is no right or wrong here. The 6 beat cycle is the most traditional where there are 6 leg kicks to each arm cycle (there are 2 arm pulls to a cycle). A 4 beat cycle is also a common pattern and a 1 beat cycle is one of the most common.

Keep in mind that most of the power to generate the movement for front crawl comes from the arms and the legs are there mainly to balance or provide a small amount of power.

For this reason a 2 beat cycle can be quite effective especially as kicking the legs at faster speeds can be very tiring. One leg kicks and one arm pulls.

What you have described is very common and with some practice you will soon have a respectful front crawl swimming stroke.

I seem to lose my front crawl technique and my kicking when I get tired. The first few lengths are ok but after that when I get tired it's all gone.

Losing your technique because of tiredness is very common and as front crawl is high energy consuming swimming stroke, it doesn't take long before it all falls apart.

A couple of things to think about that might help you out.

Firstly you mentioned your kicking. Be mindful of how much kicking you are actually doing. It is very common to kick far more than you really need to, especially over a long distance.

Remember the power and propulsion for front crawl comes mainly from the arm action. Propulsion is generated from the leg kick but no way near as much as from the arms.

Watch a long distance front crawl swimmer, for example a triathlete. Each leg kicks once for every arm pull, serving less as propulsion and more as a counter balance to the arm actions, to help keep the stroke as whole balanced and even.

On the other hand take a short distance front crawl sprint, over 50 or 100 meters. The legs kick with enormous speed and power to provide maximum propulsion and assistance to the arms with this short distance using up all energy.

Conclusion: less leg kicks equals energy saved - energy that you will need in order to swim a longer distance.

Secondly be mindful of your breathing and in particular how often you breathe. Assuming that you exhale into the water (the easiest and most natural method) and not hold your breath, which only serves to make you more tired.

72

Once again the distance being swum will dictate the frequency that you need to breathe. Longer distances more often and shorter distances less. This may sound obvious but it is all too easy to set off from the start and get the pace and frequency of the breathing wrong, despite what might feel right at the time, only for it to catch you out later in the swim.

Breathing every stroke or every other stroke will help to keep a steady pace and hopefully allow you to last longer. Bilateral breathing (alternating the side you breathe to by taking a breath every three arm pulls) is a nice even and steady breathing pattern. However even this cannot be maintained over long distances. Taking a breath every stroke cycle will cover longer distances, which again you will see if you watch any long distance swimmer.

Lastly there is the age-old problem of fitness. Your fitness and stamina will ultimately dictate how far you can swim before your body tells you it has had enough. Like any form of exercise, the more you do it the fitter and stronger you become.

Backstroke

technique overview

This is the most efficient stroke swum on the back and is the third fastest of all swimming strokes. The majority of the power is produced by the alternating arm technique and its horizontal streamlined body position gives it its efficiency. Therefore this is the preferred stroke in competitive races swum on the back.

The nature of floating on the back, face up (supine) can be a calming and relaxing feeling. Also the face is clear of the water, allowing easy breathing and little water splashes onto the face. On the other hand it can be counter productive at first, as it can give a feeling of disorientation and unease, as the person is facing upwards and therefore unaware of their surroundings. The supine body position is flat and horizontal, with ears slightly below the water surface.

The legs kick in an alternating action, continuously up and down to help balance the action of the arms. This stroke has two different arm actions: the bent arm pull, which is the most efficient, and the straight arm pull, which is the easiest to learn. Therefore the straight arm pull is best for beginners.

Breathing should be in time with recovery of each arm, breathing in with one arm recovery and out with the other. Ideally there should be 6 leg kicks to one arm cycle but the stroke timing may vary according to the swimmer's level of coordination.

Body Position

The supine body position for this stroke is flat and horizontal, with ears slightly below the water surface.

Good floaters will find this position relaxing and relatively easy, whereas poor floaters will find it difficult to achieve a comfortable head position.

Body position remains horizontal and relaxed

The head remains still throughout the stroke with the eyes looking slightly down the body at a point the swimmer is swimming away from.

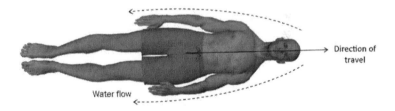

Direction of travel

Water flow

The head position is important because a raised head makes it more difficult to keep the hips raised in the correct position, which leads to a sitting type position in the water.

The hips and shoulders remain at or near the water surface but roll with the stroke. The legs and feet should be extended and remain together to maximise efficiency, with knees remaining below the water surface.

Common body position mistakes

Ever get that feeling that you are sinking when you swim on your back? It is very common to allow the legs to drop and the body position to become angled in the water without knowing it is happening. This is usually caused either by allowing the hips to drop or lifting the head slightly or a combination of both. As the legs drop deeper the whole stroke becomes less efficient and more energy consuming.

Performing a push and glide from holding the poolside is a good way of testing how flat you can remain. Ensure that you look upwards as you push away and stretch out so that your hips, legs and feet rise to the surface. The overall body position is easily maintained with a correct and efficient leg kick.

Leg Kick

During this stroke the legs kick in an alternating action, continuously up and down to help balance the action of the arms.

Legs should be stretched out with toes pointed (plantar flexed) and ankles should be relaxed and loose with toes pointing slightly inwards.

The amount of propulsion generated from the kick will depend on the size of the feet, ankle mobility and strength of the legs.

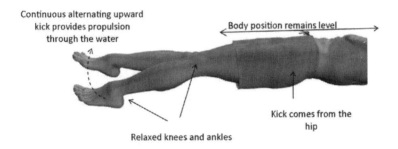

Continuous alternating upward kick provides propulsion through the water

Body position remains level

Kick comes from the hip

Relaxed knees and ankles

The knee should bend slightly and then straighten as the leg kicks upwards. Toes should kick to create a small splash but not break the water surface.

During specific leg practices the legs kick in a vertical plane. However, the arm action causes the body to roll making the legs kick part sideways, part vertical and partly to the other side.

Common leg kick mistakes

The most common fault with the leg kick during backstroke is closely related to the body position, when the swimmer allows their legs to sink below the water surface. The toes should just break the water surface and the legs kick from the hip with a slight bend at the knee.

An easy exercise to help maintain leg kick technique at the correct level in the water is to hold a float or kick board across the chest and perform the leg kick. The float will provide support so that the swimmer can focus on kicking up towards the water surface whilst maintaining a level head and level hips. Only then will the leg kick be at its most efficient.

There are two possible arm actions for backstroke. The bent arm pull, which is more effective because it is faster and has greater propulsion, and the straight arm pull used in more recreational backstroke.

Arm rises upwards, little finger leading and
arm brushing the ear

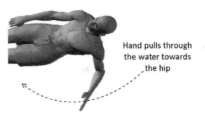

Hand pulls through
the water towards
the hip

straight arm pull

entry
The arm should be straight and as inline with the shoulder as possible. The hand should be turned with palm facing outwards and little finger entering the water first.

propulsive phase
The arm sweeps through the water in a semi-circle, pulling with force just under the water surface, pulling to the outside of the thigh.

recovery
The thumb or the back of the hand should exit the water first. The shoulders roll again with the shoulder of the recovering arm rolling upwards. The arm rotates through 180 degrees over the shoulder. The palm is turned outwards during recovery to ensure that the hand enters the water little finger first.

bent arm pull

As the arm pulls through to completion, the overall path should follow an 'S' shape.

entry
The entry is the same as the straight arm pull, with the little finger entering first, the palm facing out and the arm close to the shoulder line.

downward sweep
The palm should always face the direction of travel. The shoulders roll and the elbow bends slightly as the arm sweeps downwards and outwards.

upwards sweep
As the hand sweeps inline with the shoulder, the palm changes pitch to sweep upwards and inwards. The elbow should then bend to 9o degrees and point to the pool floor.

second downward sweep
The arm action then sweeps inwards towards the thigh and the palm faces downwards. The bent arm action is completed with the arm fully extended and the hand pushing downwards to counter balance the shoulder roll.

recovery
The thumb or the back of the hand should exit the water first. The shoulders roll again with the shoulder of the recovering arm rolling upwards. The arm rotates through 180 degrees over the shoulder. The palm is turned outwards during recovery to ensure that the hand enters the water little finger first.

Common arm pull mistakes

Two common faults cause the arms technique for backstroke to become weak and the overall stroke inefficient.

Firstly the upper arm must brush past the ear and the edge of the hand must enter the water in line with the shoulder. If the hand enters the water wide of the shoulder line then the arm pull with be incomplete and lack power.

Secondly it is very common to perform one arm pull at a time. In other words one arm completes a full arm pull cycle before the second arm begins its arm cycle. The arm pulls for backstroke should be continuous where one arm begins to pull as the other arm begins to recover.

Practicing the arm technique whilst holding a float on the chest is a good way of ensuring the hand is entering inline with the shoulder and that the arm pull is complete. Once this has been mastered then the swimmer can practice the full stroke ensuring the arms are performing continuous cycles.

Breathing during backstroke should be relaxed and easy, due to the supine body position and face being out of the water throughout the stroke. Most swimmers are neither aware of the way in which they breathe, nor the pattern of breathing or point at which a breath is taken.

Breathing should be in time with the recovery of each arm, breathing in with one arm recovery and out with the other. This encourages a breath to be taken at regular intervals.

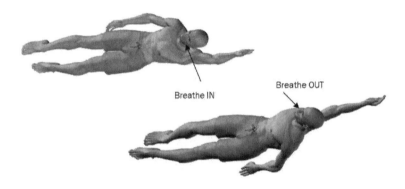

Breathe IN

Breathe OUT

A regular breathing pattern should be encouraged to prevent breath holding, particularly in beginners.

Common breathing mistakes

Breath holding is a common mistake made when swimming this stroke and the result is a very tired and breathless swimmer. Do you ever feel like you become breathless very quickly when swimming this stroke? It goes without saying that swimming contains a very large element of fitness and stamina but this is only one factor.

Breathing technique is essential and it is very common for swimmers, especially beginners to hold their breath without knowing they are doing so.

Performing the stroke slowly at first or with floats to provide support, swimmers must breathe out and then in again in time with each arm pull. Try to establish a rhythm of breathing through each stroke cycle and this will help to prevent breath holding and unnecessary tiredness and exhaustion.

An established breathing rhythm will help to maintain the timing and coordination of the arms and legs as they pull and kick. It will also assist the swimmer to relax and therefore swim with a calm, controlled and smooth backstroke.

Timing

The timing and coordination of the arms and legs develops with practice.

Ideally there should be 6 leg kicks to one arm cycle. The opposite leg kicks downwards at the beginning of each arm pull. This helps to balance the body. This may vary according to the swimmer's level of coordination.

One arm exits the water as the other begins to pull and the leg kick remains continuous

Arm action should be continuous. i.e. when one arm enters and begins to pull, the other should begin its recovery phase.

Common timing mistakes

A common mistake is performing one arm cycle at a time, resulting in an uneven and unbalanced stroke overall.

Timing and coordination problems occur with backstroke when the legs are allowed to sink below the water surface and the arms lose their continuity and pull one arm at a time.

Counting in your head can sometimes help to maintain stroke rhythm and timing. If you are able to perform a 6 beat cycle then you should count to 3 during each arm pull, therefore kicking 3 legs kicks per arm pull.

If a one beat cycle comes more naturally then there should be one leg kick for each arm pull. Performing the stroke slowly at first will help to establish the rhythm and timing and only when you are proficient swimming at a slow steady pace should you try to increase speed.

With increases in speed comes the greater potential for the timing and coordination to become disrupted and the overall swimming stroke to lose it efficiency.

Backstroke

exercises

BACKSTROKE: Body Position

Floating supine supported by floats

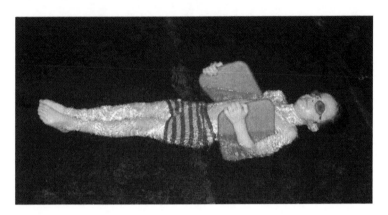

Aim: to gain confidence in a supine position on the water surface.

This exercise is ideal for the nervous swimmer. The teacher or assistant initially can provide support, if he/she is also in the water. 2 floats can then provide support, one placed under each arm, or by a woggle placed under both arms as in the photograph above.

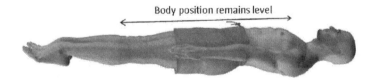

Body position remains level

Key Actions
Relax
Make your body flat on top of the water
Keep your head back
Push your tummy up to the surface
Look up to the ceiling
Keep your head still
Keep yourself in a long straight line

Technical Focus
Overall body should be horizontal and streamlined
Head remains still
Eyes looking upwards and towards the feet
Hips must be close to the surface
Legs must be together

Common Faults
Head raises out of the water
Tummy and hips sink
Failing to maintain a flat position

BACKSTROKE: Body Position

Static supine position, holding a single float

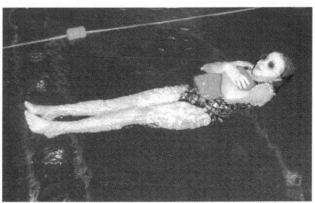

Aim: to develop confidence in a supine position.

Holding a single float across the chest gives security to the nervous swimmer, but is not as stable as a woggle or a float under each arm and so is a subtle and gradual progression. If necessary, this exercise can be performed without a float, as shown in the diagram below, as an additional progression.

Body position remains horizontal and relaxed

Key Actions

Relax
Keep your head back
Push your tummy up to the surface
Look up to the ceiling
Keep your head still

Technical Focus

Overall body should be horizontal
Head remains still
Eyes looking upwards
Hips must be close to the surface
Legs must be together

Common Faults

Head raises out of the water
Eyes look up but head tips forward
Tummy and hips sink
Head moves about
Failing to maintain a straight line

BACKSTROKE: Body Position

Push and glide holding a float

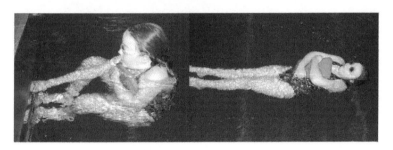

Aim: to gain confidence and move through the water in a supine position.

Holding a float gives added security to the nervous or weak swimmer whilst helping to maintain correct body position.

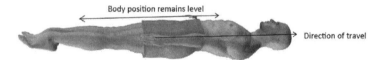

Body position remains level

Direction of travel

Float can be placed on the chest or behind the head as in the photos above.

Key Actions
Relax
Keep your head back and chin up
Push your tummy up to the surface
Look up to the ceiling
Keep your head still
Push off like a rocket

Technical Focus
Overall body should be horizontal and streamlined
Head remains still
Eyes looking upwards
Hips must be close to the surface
Legs must be together

Common Faults
Head raises out of the water
Eyes look up but head tips forward
Tummy and hips sink
Head moves about
Failing to maintain a straight line

BACKSTROKE: Body Position

Push and glide from the poolside without floats

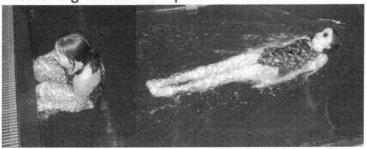

Aim: to encourage correct body position whilst moving.

The swimmer uses the momentum of a push from the poolside. Arms are held by the sides or held straight over the head in more advanced cases.

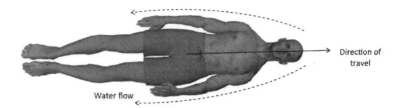

Direction of travel

Water flow

Key Actions
Relax
Make your body as long as you can
Push off like a rocket
Push your tummy up to the surface
Look up to the ceiling
Glide in a long straight line

Technical Focus
Overall body should be horizontal and streamlined
Head remains still
Eyes looking upwards and towards the feet
Hips must be close to the surface
Legs must be together
Arms are held by the sides

Common Faults
Push off is not hard enough
Head raises out of the water
Tummy and hips sink
Failing to maintain a straight line

BACKSTROKE: Legs

Static practice, sitting on the poolside

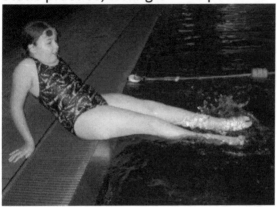

Aim: to develop an alternating leg kick action.

The swimmer is positioned sitting on the poolside with feet
in the water. This is ideal for the nervous beginner to get
accustomed to the 'feel' of the water.

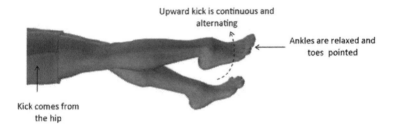

Upward kick is continuous and
alternating

Ankles are relaxed and
toes pointed

Kick comes from
the hip

Key Actions
Point your toes like a ballerina
Kick from your hips
Kick with floppy feet
Keep your legs together
Make your legs as long as possible

Technical Focus
Kick comes from the hips
Toes are pointed
Legs are together
Slight knee bend
Ankles are relaxed

Common Faults
Kick comes from the knee
Legs kick apart
Toes are turned up
Legs are too 'stiff', not relaxed

BACKSTROKE: Legs

Woggle held under the arms

Aim: to practise and develop correct leg kick action.

This exercise is ideal for the nervous beginner as an introduction to swimming on the back. The stability of the woggle encourages kicking and motion backwards with ease.

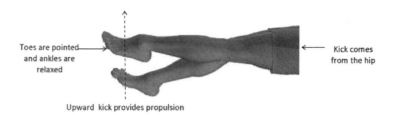

Toes are pointed and ankles are relaxed

Kick comes from the hip

Upward kick provides propulsion

Key Actions
Point your toes like a ballerina
Kick from your hips
Kick with floppy feet
Make a small splash with your toes

Technical Focus
Kick comes from the hips
Kick is alternating and continuous
Kick breaks the water surface
Hips and tummy up near the surface
Toes are pointed and ankles relaxed
Legs are together
Slight knee bend

Common Faults
Kick comes from the knee
Hips sink and legs kick too deep
Toes are turned up
Stiff ankles
Legs are too 'stiff', not relaxed

BACKSTROKE: Legs

Float held under each arm

Aim: to practise and develop leg action whilst maintaining correct body position.

Two floats provide good support and encourage a relaxed body position, without creating excessive resistance through the water.

Body alignment and direction of travel

Continuous alternating upward kick provides propulsion through the water

Key Actions

Relax and kick hard
Point your toes like a ballerina
Kick from your hips
Kick with floppy feet
Make a small splash with your toes
Keep your legs together

Technical Focus

Kick breaks the water surface
Hips and tummy are up near the surface
Toes are pointed and ankles relaxed
Legs are together
Slight knee bend
Ankles are relaxed

Common Faults

Toes are turned up, causing a lack of motion
Head comes up, causing legs to sink
Hips sink and legs kick too deep
Legs kick apart

BACKSTROKE: Legs

Float held on the chest

Aim: to allow the correct body position to be maintained whilst the legs kick.

This is a progression from having a float held under each arm. The swimmer is less stable but still has the security of one float held on the chest.

Ankles are relaxed and toes pointed to provide power to the upward kick

Body position remains level

Kick comes from the hip

Key Actions

Point your toes like a ballerina
Kick from your hips
Kick with floppy feet
Make a small splash with your toes
Keep your legs together

Technical Focus

Kick comes from the hips
Kick is alternating and continuous
Kick breaks the water surface
Hips and tummy up near the surface
Legs are together
Ankles are relaxed and toes pointed

Common Faults

Kick comes from the knee o Legs are too deep
Toes are turned up
Stiff ankles
Legs are too 'stiff', not relaxed

BACKSTROKE: Legs

Float held behind the head

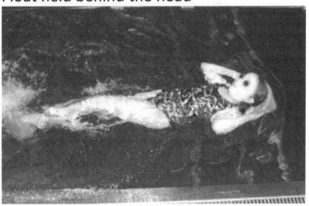

Aim: to encourage correct body position as the legs kick.

The float behind the head helps to keep the chest and hips high. A variation of the exercise with the float held on the chest, this exercise helps to develop leg strength and stamina.

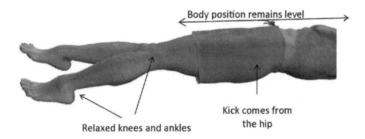

Body position remains level

Relaxed knees and ankles

Kick comes from the hip

Key Actions
Kick from your hips
Kick with floppy feet
Make a small splash with your toes
Keep your legs together

Technical Focus
Kick comes from the hips
Kick breaks the water surface
Hips and tummy up near the surface
Toes are pointed and ankles relaxed
Legs are together

Common Faults
Kick comes from the knee
Legs are too deep
Toes are turned up
Stiff ankles
Legs too 'stiff', not relaxed

BACKSTROKE: Legs

Float held over the knees

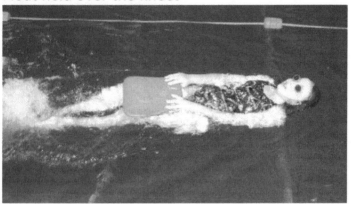

Aim: to prevent excessive knee bend by holding a float over the knees.

This kicking practice should be performed with the float held on the water surface without the knees hitting it as they kick.

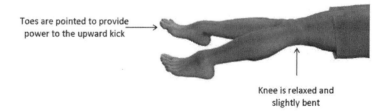

Toes are pointed to provide power to the upward kick

Knee is relaxed and slightly bent

Key Actions
Kick with straight legs
Point your toes like a ballerina
Stop your knees hitting the float
Kick with floppy feet

Technical Focus
Kick comes from the hips
Legs kick without touching the float
Kick breaks the water surface
Hips and tummy up near the surface
Toes are pointed and ankles relaxed

Common Faults
Kick comes from the knee
Knees bend and hit the float
Leg kick is too deep
Float is held up above the water surface

BACKSTROKE: Legs

Float held overhead with arms straight

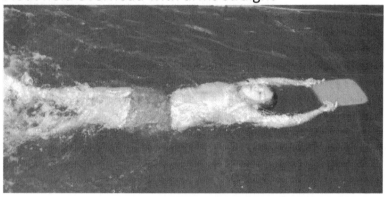

Aim: to enhance a correct body position whilst kicking.

This exercise is a progression from previous leg kick exercises and helps to develop a stronger leg kick.

Legs kick and correct body position is maintained throughout.
Note: advanced alternative is shown without holding a float.

Key Actions

Push your hips and chest up to the surface
Point your toes like a ballerina
Make your whole body long and straight
Kick from your hips
Stretch out and kick hard

Technical Focus

Kick comes from the hips
Arms remain either side of the head
Kick breaks the water surface
Hips and tummy up near the surface

Common Faults

Head is raised causing hips and legs to sink
Hips sink and legs kick too deep
Toes are turned up
Head is too far back and the upper body sinks

BACKSTROKE: Legs

Kicking with arms by the sides, hands sculling

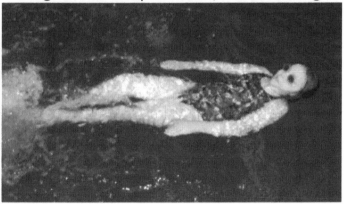

Aim: to practise kicking and maintaining correct body position.

The sculling hand action provides balance and enhances confidence.

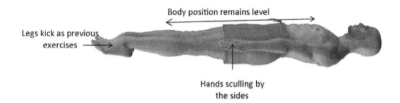

Body position remains level

Legs kick as previous exercises

Hands sculling by the sides

Key Actions
Relax
Push your hips and chest up to the surface
Point your toes like a ballerina
Kick with floppy feet
Look up to the sky

Technical Focus
Kick comes from the hips
Kick is alternating and continuous
Kick breaks the water surface
Hips and tummy up near the surface
Ankles are relaxed and toes are pointed

Common Faults
Kick comes from the knee
Hips sink and legs kick too deep
Head is too far back
Body is not relaxed

BACKSTROKE: Arms

Static practice standing on the poolside

Aim: to practise the arm action in its most basic form.

Standing on the poolside allows the swimmer to develop basic technique in a static position.

Arm rises upwards, little finger leading and arm brushing the ear

Hand pulls downwards toward the hip

Key Actions
Arms brush past your ear
Fingers closed together
Arms are continuous
Stretch your arm all the way up to your ear
Pull down to your side

Technical Focus
Arm action is continuous
Arms stretch all the way up and brush past the ear
Arms pull down to the side, towards the hip

Common Faults
Arms are not rising to touch the ear
Arms are not pulling down to the side
Pausing in-between arm pulls
Arms are bending over the head

BACKSTROKE: Arms

Single arm pull with a float held on the chest

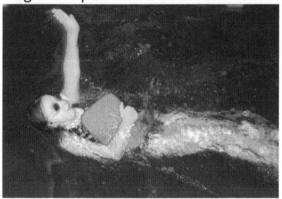

Aim: to develop correct arm action whilst kicking.

The float held on the chest provides support for the beginner and the single arm action allows easy learning without compromising the swimmer's coordination.

Arm exits the water and brushes past the ear, entering the water little finger first

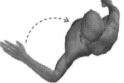

Arm is bent as it pulls through and straightens as it pulls to the thigh

Key Actions
Arm brushes past your ear
Pull down to your thigh
Fingers closed together
Little finger enters the water first

Technical Focus
Arm action is continuous
Arms stretch all the way up and brush past the ear
Arms pull down to the thigh
Fingers are together
Little finger enters water first

Common Faults
Arms are pulling out too wide, not brushing the ear
Arms are not pulling down to the side
Arms pull too deep under the water
Fingers are apart
Thumb enters the water first

BACKSTROKE: Arms

Single arm pull using the lane rope

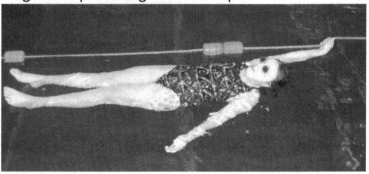

Aim: to develop a bent arm pull using the lane rope to move though the water.

The hand remains fixed on the lane rope as the body is pulled along in the line of the rope. This simulates the bent arm pull action.

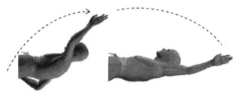

Arm exits the water and brushes past the ear, entering the water little finger first, taking hold of the lane rope

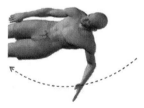

Swimmer pulls from above the head and then pushes past the hip to simulate the bent arm pull action

Key Actions

Use the rope to pull you along
Arms brush past your ear
Stretch over and hold the rope behind
Pull fast down the rope
Thumb comes out first
Little finger enters the water first

Technical Focus

Arm action is continuous
Arms stretch all the way up and brush past the ear
Arms pull down to the thigh
Arm action is continuous
Thumb comes out first

Common Faults

Arms are not pulling down to the side
Elbow is not bending enough
Arms are bending over the head
Thumb enters the water first

BACKSTROKE: Arms

Single arm pull with the opposite arm held by the side

Aim: to practise correct arm action without the aid of floats.

This single arm exercise allows focus on one arm whilst the arm held by the side encourages correct body position.

Arm rises upwards, little finger leading and arm brushing the ear

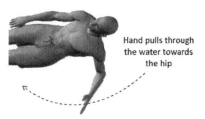

Hand pulls through the water towards the hip

Key Actions
Arms brush past your ear
Arms are continuous
Pull down to your side
Pull fast through the water
Little finger enters the water first

Technical Focus
Arm action is continuous
Arms stretch all the way up and brush past the ear
Arms pull down to the thigh
Shoulders rock with each arm pull
Little finger enters the water first

Common Faults
Arms are pulling out too wide, not brushing the ear
Arms are not pulling down to the side
Arms pull too deep under the water
Arms are bending over the head

BACKSTROKE: Arms

Arms only with pull-buoy held between legs

Aim: to develop a continual arm action using both arms.

The pull-buoy provides support and helps to isolate the arms by preventing the leg kick action. Note: it is normal for the legs to 'sway' from side to side during this exercise.

Continual arm action causes an even rocking of the shoulders

Key Actions
Arms brush past your ear
Fingers closed together
Continuous arm action
Pull hard through the water and down to your side
Allow your legs to 'sway' side to side

Technical Focus
Arm action is continuous and steady
Arms stretch all the way over and brush past the ear
Arms pull down to the thigh
Shoulders rock evenly side to side

Common Faults
Pause between arm pulls
Arms are pulling out too wide, not brushing the ear
Arms are not pulling down to the side
Arms pull too deep under the water

BACKSTROKE: Breathing

Full stroke with breathing

Aim: to focus on breathing in time with the stroke actions.

The swimmer should breathe in and out in regular rhythm with the arm action. This exercise can be incorporated into any of the previous arm action exercises, depending on the ability of the swimmer.

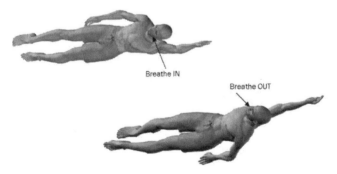

Breathe IN

Breathe OUT

Key Actions
Breathe in time with your arms
Breathe in with one arm pull and out with the other

Technical Focus
Breathing should be regular and rhythmical

Common Faults
Holding the breath
Breathing too rapidly

BACKSTROKE: Timing

Push and glide adding arms and legs

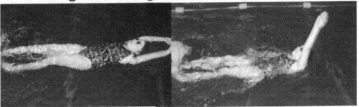

Aim: to practise and develop coordination and stroke timing.

The swimmer performs a push and glide to establish correct body position, then adds arm and leg actions.

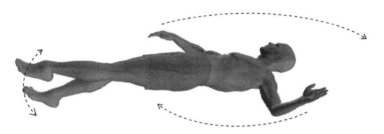

One arm exits the water as the other begins to pull and the leg kick remains continuous

Key Points

Count in your head to 3 with each arm pull
Kick 3 times with each arm pull
Keep the arm pull continuous
Keep the leg kick continuous

Technical Focus

3 leg kicks per arm pull
Leg kick should be continuous
Arm action should be regular

Common Faults

One leg kick per arm pull ('one beat cycle')
Continuous leg kick but not enough arm pulls
Arm pull is too irregular
Stroke cycle is not regular and continuous

BACKSTROKE

Full stroke

Aim: to demonstrate full stroke backstroke showing continuous and alternating arm and leg actions, with correct timing, resulting in a smooth and efficient stroke.

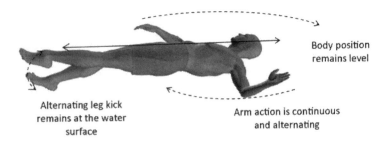

Body position remains level

Alternating leg kick remains at the water surface

Arm action is continuous and alternating

Key Actions

Kick from your hips
Relax
Keep your hips and tummy at the surface
Make a small splash with your toes
Continuous arm action
Arms brush past your ear and pull to your side

Technical Focus

Body position should be horizontal and flat
Leg kick should be continuous and alternating
Arm action is continuous
Leg kick breaks the water surface
3 legs kicks per arm pull

Common Faults

Hips and abdomen sink
Legs kick too deep or weak
Arms pull one at a time
Arms pull too wide or too deep

Backstroke

common questions

Problems and difficulties come from the fact that swimming on your back means you cannot see where you are going! Sounds obvious but when we swim in a prone position (on our front facing forwards) we can see around us and therefore are totally aware of our surroundings. Swimming along whilst facing the sky and we lose most of our surrounding awareness.

Without knowing we then lift our head slightly and this instantly causes the hips to drop and then the legs and the rest of the body follow on, the result: that sinking feeling.

How do I prevent myself from sinking?

When swimming backstroke ensure your head is back enough that your ears are submerged. Then stretch out so that your hips, legs and feet come to the surface. Your leg kick should break the water surface enough to produce a small splash.

Do not fall into the trap of trying at look for your feet or at your flat body position. Moving your head only the slightest inch to check will instantly result in that sinking feeling again. If you can feel your toes breaking the water surface then the chances are your body position is somewhere near correct.

How do I relax on my back and why do I not float when swimming backstroke?

Floating is a characteristic of the human body. Some of us float well and some of us simply do not. It is all down to relative density. Basically fat floats and muscle sinks, which is why lean or muscular people tend to sink.

Focus on your backstroke swimming technique and remaining in the correct position at the water surface will take care of itself.

Become more relaxed in a supine position (on your back) in the water by floating in a star position, with arms and legs wide. This wide body position help you to remain afloat and therefore relax. Even if you are a poor floater, the ability to relax will help all aspect of your backstroke swimming.

Breaststroke

technique overview

Breaststroke is the oldest and slowest of the four swimming strokes. It is also the most inefficient of all strokes, which is what makes it the slowest. Propulsion from the arms and legs is a consecutive action that takes place under the water. A large frontal resistance area is created as the heels draw up towards the seat and the breathing technique inclines the body position also increasing resistance. These are the main reasons that make breaststroke inefficient and slow.

This stroke is normally one of the first strokes to be taught, especially to adults, as the head and face is clear of the water, giving the swimmer a greater perception of their whereabouts and their buoyancy. There are variations in the overall technique, ranging from a slow recreational style to a more precise competitive style. Body position should be as flat and streamlined as possible with an inclination from the head to the feet so that the leg kick recovery takes place under the water.

The leg kick as a whole should be a simultaneous and flowing action, providing the majority of the propulsion.

The arm action should also be simultaneous and flowing and overall provides the smallest propulsive phase of the four strokes.

The stroke action gives a natural body lift, which gives the ideal breathing point with each stroke. A streamlined body position during the timing sequence of the arm and leg action is essential to capitalise on the propulsive phases of the stroke.

Body Position

The body position should be inclined slightly downwards from the head to the feet.

The body should be as flat and streamlined as possible with an inclination from the head to the feet so that the leg kick recovery takes place under the water.

Head movement should be kept to a minimum and the shoulders should remain level throughout the stroke

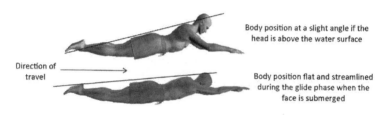

Body position at a slight angle if the head is above the water surface

Direction of travel

Body position flat and streamlined during the glide phase when the face is submerged

The main aim should be good streamlining, however the underwater recovery movements of the arms and legs together with the lifting of the head to breathe, all compromise the overall body position. In order to reduce resistance created by these movements, as the propulsive phase of an arm pull or leg kick takes place, the opposite end of the body remains still and streamlined.

Common body position mistakes

The most common mistake with the body position for breaststroke is being too flat in the water. In other words the face is submerged too much causing the hips, legs and feet to rise to the surface. This could then making lifting the face to the front to breathe more difficult. It could also lead to the feet breaking the surface of the water as they kick and therefore losing power.

The angled body position can be perfected with a simple push and glide exercise. Push and glide from the poolside either holding a float or without, but with the head and face up above the water surface.

Leg Kick

The most important teaching aspect of the legs is that the action is a series of movements that flow together to make one sweeping leg kicking action

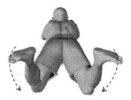

Heels are drawn up towards the seat. Soles face upwards

Feet turn outwards to allow the heels and soles to aid propulsion

Heels push back and outwards in a whip-like action

It is more important for a swimmer or teacher to recognise the difference between the wedge kick and the whip kick in breaststroke. The leg action provides the largest amount of propulsion in the stroke and swimmers will favour a wedge kick or a whip kick depending on which comes most naturally. For a whip kick, the legs kick in a whip-like action with the knees remaining close together. For a wedge kick the legs kick in a wider, more deliberate circular path.

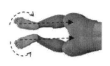

Heels drawn towards the seat and feet turn out

Heels drive back in a circular whip like action giving the kick power and motion

Kick finishes in a streamlined position with legs straight and toes pointed

139

The leg kick as a whole should be a simultaneous and flowing action, providing the majority of the propulsion. Knees bend as the heels are drawn up towards the seat and toes are turned out ready for the heels and soles of the feet to drive the water backwards. The legs sweep outwards and downwards in a flowing circular path, accelerating as they kick and return together and straight, providing a streamlined position.

Common leg kick mistakes

The feet cause most of the problems when it comes to kicking. Failure to turn the feet out will result in a lack of power and that feeling of going nowhere. Failure to turn out both feet and only turning out one foot will result in something known as a screw kick. This is where one leg kicks correctly and the other swings around providing no propulsion at all.

The best exercise for correcting theses common faults is to swim on your back (supine) with a woggle or noodle held under the arms for support. Then the swimmer is able to sit up slightly and watch their own leg kick as they perform it. Kicking in slow motion at first making a conscious effort to turn out both feet and ensure both legs and feet are symmetrical is best before attempting to add power.

Arms

The amount of propulsion generated from arm technique has developed over the years as the stroke has changed to become more competitive. The arm action overall provides the smallest propulsive phase of the four competitive strokes.

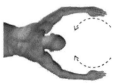

Elbows tuck in and arms and hands stretch forward into a glide

Arms and hands pull around and downwards

Catch

The arm action begins with the arms fully extended out in front, fingers and hands together. The hands pitch outwards and downwards to an angle of about 45 degrees at the start of the catch phase. The arms pull outwards and downwards until they are approximately shoulder width apart. Elbows begin to bend and shoulders roll inwards at the end of the catch phase.

Propulsive phase

The arms sweep downwards and inwards and the hands pull to their deepest point. Elbows bend to 90 degrees and remain high. At the end of the down sweep, the hands sweep inwards and slightly upwards. Elbows tuck into the sides as the hands are pulled inwards towards the chest and the chin.

Recovery

The hands recover by stretching forwards in a streamlined position. Hands recover under, on or over the water surface, depending on the style of stroke to be taught.

Common arm pull mistakes

The arm technique for this stroke usually becomes the dominant force when it should not. It is very common for swimmers to put more effort into pulling themselves through the water, when it should be the leg kick providing the power and momentum.

In an attempt to haul them through the water the arm pull is too big and too wide. It is not uncommon to pull arms completely to the side, making for an inefficient recovery under the water surface, which will almost certainly result in the swimmer slowing down.

An easy exercise to practice to help perfect the arm pull technique is to walk slowly through shallow water of about shoulder depth, ensuring the arms pull in small circles and the hands remain in front of the swimmer at all times. They should also extend forwards and remain there momentarily for the glide phase.

Breathing

Breaststroke has a natural body lift during the stroke, which gives the ideal breathing point during each stroke cycle.

Inhalation takes place at the end of the arm in sweep as the body allows the head to lift clear of the water. The head should be lifted enough for the mouth to clear the surface and inhale, but not excessively so as to keep the frontal resistance created by this movement to a minimum.

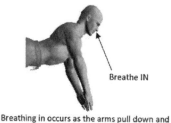

Breathing in occurs as the arms pull down and the head rises above the surface

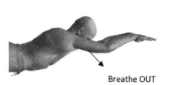

Breathing out occurs as the arms recover out in front

Explosive or trickle breathing can be utilised.

The head returns to the water to exhale as the arms stretch forward to begin their recovery phase.

Some swimmers perform the stroke with the head raised throughout to keep the mouth and nose clear of the water at all times. This simplifies the breathing but at the expense of a greater frontal resistance.

Common breathing mistakes

Some beginners experience difficulty breathing during breaststroke. The two main reasons are failing to lift the head enough to clear the water surface and breathe, and holding the breath and therefore failing to breathe out into the water.

Breaststroke needs a powerful leg kick and it is this leg kick that gives a natural body lift. Together with the arm action there should be enough lift to enable the mouth to clear the water surface for inhalation to take place.

The most common mistake made with breaststroke breathing is failing to exhale during the glide phase making it impossible to inhale again, or forcing the swimmer to use an explosive breathing technique.

Although explosive breathing is a valid breathing technique for this swimming stroke, it is usually only used competitively.

When swum recreationally, exhaling during the glide phase of the stroke is more efficient and uses less energy.

Using a woggle under the arms provides support and allows the swimmer to swim in slow motion whilst practicing the breathing technique. Extending the body into a long glide as exhalation takes place ensures the breathing takes place at the time that keeps the stroke at its most efficient.

Timing

The coordination of the propulsive phases should be a continuous alternating action, where one propulsive phase takes over as one ends. The stroke timing can be summed up with the following sequence: pull, breath, kick, glide.

A streamlined body position at the end of that sequence is essential to capitalise on the propulsive phases of the stroke. The timing can be considered in another way: when the arms are pulling in their propulsive phase, the legs are streamlined and when the legs are kicking in propulsion, the arms are streamlined.

Body position starts with hands and feet together

Pull, breathe, kick, glide sequence is performed

Swimmer returns to original body position.

Full body extension is essential before the start of each stroke cycle.

Decreasing or even eliminating the glide and using the arm and leg actions in an almost continuous stroke to give more propulsion are a more competitive variation of stroke timing.

Common timing mistakes

As this stoke is a simultaneous stroke it is very common to kick with the legs and pull with the arms at the same time. The result will be a very inefficient swimming stroke as the arms and legs counter act each other.

To ensure the timing and coordination of the arms and legs are correct the swimmer must focus on performing an arm pull followed by a leg kick, or on 'kicking their hands forwards'. In other words as their legs kick round and back, their arms must extend forwards. This ensures that the arms and legs are working efficiently and are extended out together during the glide phase.

Breaststroke

exercises

BREASTSTROKE: Body Position

Push and glide

 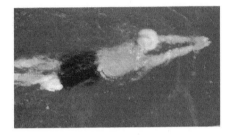

Aim: to develop a basic body position by pushing from the side

The distance of the glide will be limited due to the resistance created by the chest and shoulders. The exercise can be performed with the face submerged as it would be during the glide phase of the stroke or with the head up facing forwards.

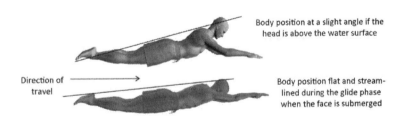

Body position at a slight angle if the head is above the water surface

Direction of travel

Body position flat and stream-lined during the glide phase when the face is submerged

Key Actions

Push hard from the side
Keep head up looking forward
Stretch out as far as you can
Keep your hands together
Keep your feet together

Technical Focus

Head remains still and central
Face is up so that only the chin is in the water
Eyes are looking forwards over the surface
Shoulders should be level and square
Hips are slightly below shoulder level
Legs are in line with the body

Common Faults

Shoulders and/or hips are not level
Head is not central and still
One shoulder is in front of the other

BREASTSTROKE: Legs

Sitting on the poolside with feet in the water

Aim: to practice the leg action whilst sat stationary on the poolside.

This exercise allows the pupil to copy the teacher who can also be sat on the poolside demonstrating the leg kick. The physical movement can be learnt before attempting the leg kick in the water.

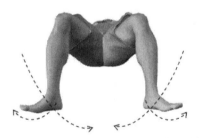

Feet turn out as the legs begin to kick round in a circular action

Key Actions

Kick your legs simultaneously

Keep your knees close together

Kick like a frog

Make sure your legs are straight and together at the end of the
kick

Technical Focus

Kick should be simultaneous

Legs should be a mirror image

Heels are drawn towards the seat

The feet turn out just before the kick

Feet come together at the end of the kick with legs straight and
toes pointed

Common Faults

Circular kick in the opposite direction

Only turning one foot out

Legs are not straight at the end of the kick

Leg action is not circular

BREASTSTROKE: Legs

Supine position with a woggle held under the arms

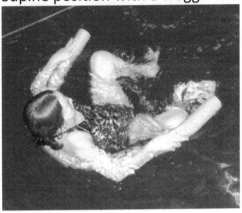

Aim: to develop breaststroke leg kick in a supine position.

This allows the swimmer to see their legs kicking. The woggle provides stability for the beginner and, with the swimmer in a supine position, allows the teacher easy communication during the exercise.

Heels drive back in a circular whip like action giving the kick power and motion

Kick finishes in a streamlined position with legs straight and toes pointed

Key Actions

Kick with both legs at the same time
Keep your feet in the water
Kick like a frog
Kick and glide
Point your toes at the end of the kick

Technical Focus

Kick should be simultaneous
Heels are drawn towards the seat
The feet turn out just before the kick
Feet kick back with knees just inline with the hips
Feet come together at the end of the kick

Common Faults

Feet are coming out of the water
Failing to bring the heels up to the bottom
Leg kick is not simultaneous
Legs are not straight at the end of the kick

BREASTSTROKE: Legs

Static practice holding the poolside

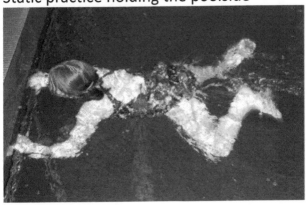

Aim: to practise breaststroke leg action in a static position.

This allows the swimmer to develop correct technique in a prone position in the water. Kicking WITHOUT force and power should be encouraged during this exercise to avoid undue impact on the lower back.

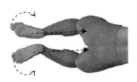

Heels drawn towards the seat and feet turn out

Heels draw round in a circular motion

Key Actions

Kick both legs at the same time

Kick like a frog

Draw a circle with your heels

Make sure your legs are straight at the end of the kick

Technical Focus

Legs should be a mirror image

Heels are drawn towards the seat

The feet turn out just before the kick

Feet kick back with knees inline with the hips

Feet come together at the end of the kick with legs straight and
toes pointed

Common Faults

Only turning one foot out

Legs are not simultaneous

Leg action is not circular

BREASTSTROKE: Legs

Prone position with a float held under each arm

Aim: to practise and develop correct leg technique in a prone position.

Using two floats aids balance and stability and encourages correct body position whilst moving through the water.

Heels are drawn up towards the seat. Soles face upwards

Feet turn outwards to allow the heels and soles to aid propulsion

Heels push back and outwards in a whip-like action

Key Actions
Keep your knees close together
Point your toes to your shins
Drive the water backwards with your heels
Glide with legs straight at the end of the each kick

Technical Focus
Leg kick should be simultaneous
Heels are drawn towards the seat
The feet turn out just before the kick
Feet kick back with knees inline with the hips
Feet come together at the end of the kick

Common Faults
One foot turns out, causing a 'scissor' like kick
Legs kick back and forth
Legs kick is not simultaneous
Toes are not pointed at the end of the kick

BREASTSTROKE: Legs

Holding a float out in front with both hands

Aim: to practise and learn correct kicking technique and develop leg strength. Holding a single float or kickboard out in front isolates the legs and creates a slight resistance which demands a stronger kick with which to maintain momentum.

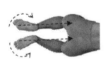

Heels drawn towards the seat and feet turn out

Heels drive back in a circular whip like action giving the kick power and motion

Kick finishes in a streamlined position with legs straight and toes pointed

Key Actions

Drive the water backwards with force
Turn your feet out and drive the water with your heels
Kick and glide
Kick like a frog
Make your feet like a penguin

Technical Focus

Kick should be simultaneous
Legs drive back to provide momentum
Heels are drawn towards the seat
The feet turn out before the kick
Feet come together at the end of the kick with legs straight and
toes pointed

Common Faults

Kick is slow and lacking power
Failing to bring the heels up to the bottom
Feet are breaking the water surface
Toes are not pointed at the end of the kick

BREASTSTROKE: Legs

Arms stretched out in front holding a float vertically

Aim: to develop leg kick strength and power.

The float held vertically adds resistance to the movement and requires the swimmer to kick with greater effort. This exercise is ideal for strengthening with a weak leg kick.

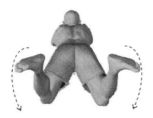

Heels push back and outwards in a whip-like action

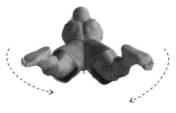

Heels drive back to add power to the kick

Key Actions

Kick your legs simultaneously

Push the water with your heels and the soles of your feet

Drive the water backwards with your heels

Technical Focus

Arms should be straight and float should be held partly underwater

Kick should be a whip like action

Feet kick back with knees inline with the hips

Feet come together at the end of the kick

Common Faults

Float is held flat or out of the water

Not turning both feet out

Leg kick lacks sufficient power

BREASTSTROKE: Legs

Supine position with hands held on hips

Aim: to develop leg kick strength and stamina.

This exercise is more advanced and requires the leg kick to be previously well practised.

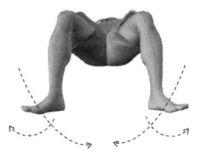

Feet turn out as the legs begin to kick round in a circular action

Key Actions
Keep your feet in the water
Kick like a frog
Make sure your legs are straight after each kick
Kick and glide
Point your toes at the end of the kick

Technical Focus
Kick should be simultaneous
Heels are drawn towards the seat
The feet turn out just before the kick
Feet kick back with knees inline with the hips
Feet come together at the end of the kick with legs straight and
    toes pointed

Common Faults
Not turning both feet out
Kick is not hard enough to provide power
Legs are not straight at the end of the kick
Toes are not pointed at the end of the kick

BREASTSTROKE: Legs

Moving practice with arms stretched out in front

Aim: to practise correct kicking technique and develop leg strength

This is an advanced exercise as holding the arms out in front demands a stronger kick with which to maintain momentum whilst maintaining a streamlined body position.

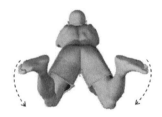

Heels push back and outwards in a whip-like action

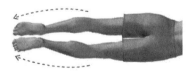

Kick finishes in a streamlined position with legs straight and toes pointed

Key Actions
Keep your knees close together
Drive the water with your heels
Make sure your legs are straight at the end of the kick
Kick and glide

Technical Focus
Kick should be simultaneous
The feet turn out just before the kick
Feet kick back with knees just inline with the hips
Feet come together at the end of the kick with legs straight and
    toes pointed

Common Faults
Not turning both feet out
Feet are breaking the water surface
Legs are not straight at the end of the kick
Toes are not pointed at the end of the kick

BREASTSTROKE: Arms

Static practice standing on the poolside

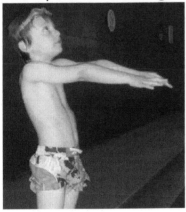 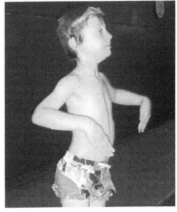

Aim: to learn the arm pull technique in its most basic form.

On the poolside, either sitting or standing, the swimmer can practise and perfect the movement without the resistance of the water.

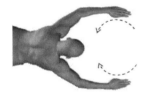

Arms and hands pull around and downwards

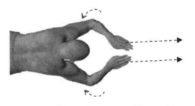

Elbows tuck in and arms extend forward

Key Actions
Both arms pull at the same time
Keep your fingers closed together
Keep your hands flat
Tuck your elbows into your sides after each pull
Stretch your arms forward until they are straight
Draw an upside down heart with your hands

Technical Focus
Arm action should be simultaneous
Fingers should be together
Arm pull should be circular
Elbows should be tucked in after each pull
Arms should extend forward and together after each pull

Common Faults
Fingers apart
Arms pull at different speeds
Arms pull past the shoulders
Elbows fail to tuck in each time
Arms fail to extend full forward

BREASTSTROKE: Arms

Walking practice moving through shallow water

Aim: to practise and develop correct arm technique from in the water.

The swimmer can experience the feel of pulling the water whilst walking along the pool floor. Where the water is too deep, this exercise can be performed standing on the poolside. Submerging the face is optional at this stage.

Arms and hands pull back in a circular motion

Elbows tuck in and arms and hands stretch forward into a glide

Key Actions
Pull with both arms at the same time
Keep your hands under the water
Tuck your elbows into your sides after each pull
Stretch your arms forward until they are straight
Draw an upside down heart with your hands

Technical Focus
Arm action should be simultaneous
Arms and hands should remain under water
Fingers should be together
Arms should extend forward and together until straight after
    each pull

Common Faults
Fingers are apart
Arms pull past the shoulders
Elbows fail to tuck in each time
Arms fail to extend full forward
Hands come out of the water

BREASTSTROKE: Arms

Moving practice with a woggle held under the arms

Aim: to learn correct arm action whilst moving through the water.

The use of the woggle means that leg kicks are not required to assist motion and this then helps develop strength in the arm pull. The woggle slightly restricts arm action but not enough to negate the benefits of this exercise.

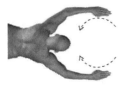

Arms and hands pull around
and downwards

Elbows tuck in and arms and hands stretch
forward into a glide

Key Actions
Pull round in a circle
Keep your hands under the water
Keep your fingers together and hands flat
Pull your body through the water
Draw an upside down heart with your hands

Technical Focus
Arm action should be simultaneous
Arms and hands should remain under water
Arms and hands should extend forward after the pull
Fingers should be together
Arm pull should be circular

Common Faults
Fingers are apart
Arms fail to extend fully forward
Hands come out of the water
Arms extend forward too far apart

BREASTSTROKE: Arms

Arms only with a pull-buoy held between the legs

Aim: to develop strength in the arm pull.

The pull-buoy prevents the legs from kicking, therefore isolating the arms. As the legs are stationary, forward propulsion and a glide action is difficult and therefore the arm action is made stronger as it has to provide all the propulsion for this exercise.

Arms and hands pull back in a circular motion

Elbows tuck in and arms and hands stretch forward together

Key Actions

Keep your hands under the water
Pull your body through the water
Keep your elbows high as you pull
Tuck your elbows into your sides after each pull
Stretch your arms forward until they are straight

Technical Focus

Arms and hands should remain under water
Arm pull should be circular
Elbows should be tucked in after each pull
Arms should extend forward and together

Common Faults

Arms pull past the shoulders
Elbows fail to tuck in each time
Arms fail to extend full forward
Hands come out of the water
Arms extend forward too far apart

BREASTSTROKE: Arms

Push and glide adding arm pulls

Aim: to progress arm action and technique from previous exercises

By incorporating a push and glide, this allows the swimmer to practise maintaining a correct body position whilst using the arms. This is a more advanced exercise as the number of arms pulls and distance travelled will vary according to the strength of the swimmer.

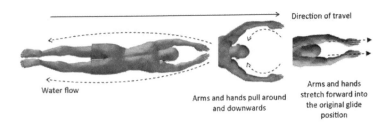

Direction of travel

Water flow

Arms and hands pull around and downwards

Arms and hands stretch forward into the original glide position

Key Actions

Keep your hands under the water
Pull your body through the water
Tuck your elbows into your sides after each pull
Stretch your arms forward with hands together

Technical Focus

Arms and hands should remain under water
Elbows should be tucked in after each pull
Arms should extend forward into a glide position
Body position should be maintained throughout

Common Faults

Arms pull past the shoulders
Arms fail to extend full forward
Hands come out of the water
Arms extend forward too far apart
Arms fail to bend during the pull

BREASTSTROKE: Breathing

Static practice, breathing with arm action

Aim: to practise breaststroke breathing action whilst standing in the water.

This allows the swimmer to experience the feel of breathing into the water in time with the arm action, without the need to actually swim.

Breathe IN as the arms pull down and the head rises

Breathe OUT as the arms recover forward and the face enters the water

Key Actions
Breathe in as you complete your arm pull
Breathe out as your hands stretch forwards
Blow your hands forwards

Technical Focus
Breath inwards at the end of the in sweep
Head lifts up as the arms complete the pull
Head should clear the water
Head returns to the water as the arms recover
Breath out is as the hands recover forward

Common Faults
Head fails to clear the water
Breathing out as the arms pull back
Lifting the head to breathe as the arms recover

BREASTSTROKE: Breathing

Breathing practice with woggle under the arms

Aim: to develop correct synchronisation of breathing and arm pull technique.

The woggle provides support, which enables the exercise to be done slowly at first. It also allows the swimmer to travel during the practice. Leg action can be added if necessary. Note: the woggle can restrict complete arm action.

Breathe IN

Breathing in occurs as the arms pull down and the head rises above the surface

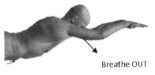

Breathe OUT

Breathing out occurs as the arms recover out in front

Key Actions

Breathe in as you complete your arm pull
Breathe out as your hands stretch forwards
Blow your hands forwards

Technical Focus

Breath inwards at the end of the in-sweep
Head lifts up as the arms complete the pull back
Head should clear the water
Head returns to the water as the arms recover
Breathing out is as the hands stretch forward

Common Faults

Holding the breath
Head fails to clear the water
Breathing out as the arms pull back
Lifting the head as the arms stretch forward

BREASTSTROKE: Breathing

Float held in front, breathing with leg kick

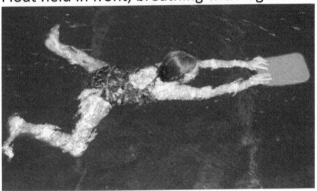

Aim: to develop the breathing technique in time with the leg kick.

The float provides stability and allows the swimmer to focus on the breathe, kick, glide sequence.

Breathe IN just before the knees bend for the kick

Breathe OUT as the legs kick into a glide

Key Actions

Breathe in as your legs bend ready to kick
Breathe out as you kick and glide
Kick your head down

Technical Focus

Inward breathing should be just before the knees bend
Head lifts up as the knees bend ready to kick
Mouth should clear the water
Head returns to the water as the legs thrust backwards
Breathe out is as the legs kick into a glide

Common Faults

Holding the breath
Head fails to clear the water
Breathing out as the knees bend ready to kick
Lifting the head as the legs kick into a glide

BREASTSTROKE: Timing

Slow practice with woggle under the arms

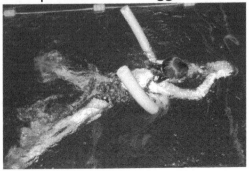

Aim: to practise the stroke timing in its most basic form.

The use of the woggle placed under the arms allows the swimmer to practice the exercise in stages as slowly as they need. It must be noted that the woggle resists against the glide and therefore the emphasis must be placed on the timing of the arms and legs. The glide can be developed using other exercises.

Body position starts with hands and feet together

Pull, breathe, kick, glide sequence is performed

Swimmer returns to original body position.

Key Actions
Pull with your hands first
Kick your hands forwards
Kick your body into a glide
Pull, breathe, kick, glide

Technical Focus
From a streamlined position arms should pull first
Legs should kick into a glide
Legs should kick as the hands and arms recover
A glide should precede the next arm pull

Common Faults
Kicking and pulling at the same time
Failure to glide
Legs kick whilst gliding

BREASTSTROKE: Timing

Push and glide, adding stroke cycles

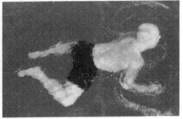

Aim: to practise and develop correct stroke timing.

The swimmer starts with a push and glide to establish a streamlined glide. The arm pull, breath in and then leg kick is executed in the correct sequence, resulting in another streamlined glide.

Push and glide to establish body position   Pull, breathe, kick and glide again

Key Actions
Kick your hands forwards
Kick your body into a glide
Pull, breathe, kick, glide

Technical Focus
From a streamlined position arms should pull first
Legs should kick into a glide
Legs should kick as the hands and arms recover
A glide should precede the next arm pull

Common Faults
Kicking and pulling at the same time
Failure to glide
Legs kick whilst gliding

BREASTSTROKE: Timing

Two kicks, one arm pull

Aim: to perfect timing whilst maintaining a streamlined body position.

From a push and glide, the swimmer performs a 'pull, breathe, kick, glide' stroke cycle into another streamlined glide. They then perform an additional kick whilst keeping the hands and arms stretched out in front. This encourages concentration on timing and coordination and at the same time develops leg kick strength.

A full stroke cycle is performed from a push and glide

Additional kick whilst the hands and arms remain still

Key Actions
Kick your body into a glide
Pull, breathe, kick, glide

Technical Focus
Legs should kick into a glide
Legs should kick as the hands and arms recover
A glide should follow each leg kick
Head lifts to breath with each arm pull

Common Faults
Arms pull too often and too early
Failure to glide
Failure to keep the hands together for the second kick

BREASTSTROKE
Full stroke

Aim: to swim full stroke Breast Stroke demonstrating efficient arm and leg action, with regular breathing and correct timing.

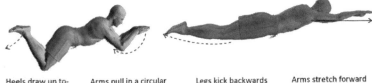

Heels draw up towards the seat and feet turn out

Arms pull in a circular action and elbows tuck in

Legs kick backwards providing power and propulsion

Arms stretch forward into a glide

Key Actions

Kick and glide
Kick your hands forwards
Drive your feet backward through the water
Keep your fingers together and under the water
Pull in a small circle then stretch forward
Breath with each stroke

Technical Focus

Head remains still and central
Shoulders remain level
Leg kick is simultaneous
Feet turn out and drive backwards
Arm action should be circular and simultaneous
Breathing is regular with each stroke cycle

Common Faults

Failure to glide
Stroke is rushed
Leg kick is not simultaneous
Arms pull to the sides
Failing to breath regularly

Breaststroke

common questions

I would like some tips on how to swim breaststroke with more speed. Which parts of my breaststroke technique could I change to gain more speed?

The propulsion for breaststroke comes from having a powerful leg kick, but speed over a longer distance comes from the glide phase of the stroke.

Firstly develop the power and technique of your leg kick by kicking whilst holing onto a float or kick board. Ensure your leg kick is complete by bringing your feet together and straightening out your legs at the end of each kick phase. Each kick should be a powerful whip action, keeping your knees relatively close together.

The power and strength of your leg kick can be enhanced and improved by holding the float in a vertical position in the water. This will add frontal resistance and make the exercise more intense and therefore will force your legs to have to kick with more power and work harder.

Next ensure that your arms are fully extended at the end of each arm pull phase. The circular motion of the arm action should be a small circle just in front of you. A common mistake is to pull wide and allow the hands to pull past the shoulders. Fully extending the arms and hands after each arm pull will ensure that the maximum distance is covered with each stroke.

Correct timing ensures an effective glide phase. The glide phase occurs just after the legs kick back and round and arms extend forward. Wait momentarily and glide to a second or two with arms together and feet together in a streamlined position in the water.

A good swimming exercise for improving breaststroke timing and body position is to swim using two leg kicks and one arm pull cycles. In other words swim a breaststroke cycle normally (pull, breathe, kick, glide) and then hold the glide position with the arms and add an additional leg kick.

You can experiment with gliding for different lengths of time. The longer the glide, the less strokes it will take to get to the end of the pool, but glide for too long and you will slow down and lose momentum.

Competitive breaststroke contains virtually no glide phase, as the arms pull as soon as the leg kick is complete. The speed of the stroke comes from the power and strength of the arm pull and the leg kick, combined with the arms and legs fully extending to gain as much distance per stroke cycle as possible.

A combination of all of the above tips and exercises will help make your breaststroke faster.

Will I lose weight swimming breaststroke? I want to start swimming for weight loss and the most enjoyable style for me is the breaststroke. But, I don't like to put my face in the water.

Swimming breaststroke without putting your face in the water is probably one of the most common ways of swimming. The fact that it is technically incorrect is of no importance if that is the way you wish to swim.

If weight loss is your goal then go for it. Swimming is arguably one of the best ways of burning calories, toning your muscles and changing your body shape. But keep one very important thing in mind...

Swimming is easy to take it easy. If you plod up and down the pool at a gentle pace it will not be a challenge to your body. You will then burn very little calories and the result will be little or no weight loss.

So, you absolutely must take yourself out of your comfort zone. In other words get out of breath in the same way you would if you were to do a workout at the gym. To achieve this in the pool simply try swimming one length as fast as you can followed by a slower length to recover. Repeat this as many times as you can for at least 20 minutes.

As you become fitter and your weight goes down you will find it easy again, so change the pattern. Maybe do 2 lengths at speed and only one to recover. Maybe take a float and just use your legs to give them a workout. Maybe try one length full speed, one medium pace and then one slow.

There are hundreds of ways of varying your swimming even if you only swim one stroke one way. The point is to keep it challenging for your body and at the same time it remains interesting. Also your weight loss is less likely to plateau and your fitness and body shape will continue change the way you want it to.

Why do my legs sink whenever I swim breaststroke? Is it because my kick is not strong enough?

You could be right in your assumption that your breaststroke leg kick is not strong or powerful enough and that is the cause of your legs sinking as you swim.

The power of the kick is vital for maintaining the movement and momentum of the stroke and the majority of the drive of the stroke should come from the leg kick. Correct body position and a smooth glide will also help maintain momentum and reduce or prevent your legs sinking.

Ensure that when you kick, you drive you heels back and around in a whip-like action. The surface area of the underside of each foot and your heel should be facing backwards as if pushing away from the pool wall. That way they can push on the water to provide maximum power.

To help strengthen your leg kick, try kicking whilst holding a kick board or float. Hold the kick board in both hands with arms out straight in front of you. Try not to bare your weight on the kick board at all. Instead relax and allow it to float.

If you find this tricky then you can try the exercise with two kick boards, one held under each arm.

Do not be put off if you feel you are not moving at all. The kick boards provide resistance to the front and therefore they are an excellent way of helping to increase leg kick strength.

After each whip-like leg kick, the feet should then be pointed backwards and inline to provide a streamlined shape as they glide. If the feet remain turned out or toes remain turned up after the legs come together they will cause drag and almost certainly sink.

If possible ensure you submerge you face with each stroke, or at least keep you chin on the water surface and eyes facing forwards and not upwards. This will encourage and flatter and therefore more streamlined body position.

Although breaststroke can be swum with the body at an angle in the water, if the angle is too steep then this results in increased frontal resistance. Combine this with a weak leg kick and you really will go nowhere fast!

Butterfly

technique overview

Butterfly stroke is the most recent stroke, developed in the 1950's, and it is the second fastest stroke to Front Crawl. The stroke evolved from breaststroke as it also contains a simultaneous leg action and simultaneous arm action. The stroke requires a great deal of upper body strength and can be very physically demanding; therefore it is a stroke that is swum competitively rather than recreationally.

Buoyancy is very important because the arms are recovered over the water and the head is raised to breathe, therefore good floaters will achieve this far easier than poor floaters.

The timing and coordination of the stroke is usually a two beat cycle of leg kicks to one arm cycle.

The undulating action of the body and the legs create great demands of the spine, therefore there are many alternative exercises and practices that can be used to make learning the stroke easier and less physical.

Breathing is an explosive exhalation and then inhalation in the short second that the head and face are above the water surface.

The timing and coordination of butterfly is usually a two beat cycle of leg kicks to one arm cycle. One leg kick should have enough power to assist the upper body out and over the water surface and the second leg kick to assist the arms as they recover just over the surface of the water.

Body Position

The body position varies through the stroke cycle due to the continuous undulating action. The body should undulate from head to toe, producing a dolphin-type action.

Although undulation is unavoidable, the body position should be kept as horizontal as possible to keep frontal resistance to a minimum. Intermittent or alternative breathing will help to maintain this required body position.

The body should be face down (prone) with the crown of the head leading the action.

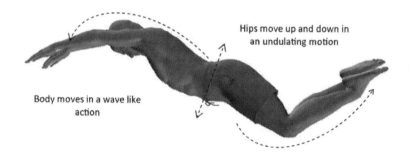

Hips move up and down in an undulating motion

Body moves in a wave like action

The shoulders should remain level throughout and the head should remain central and still, looking down until breathing is required.

Hips should be inline with the shoulders and should remain parallel to the direction of travel.

Common body position mistakes

The most common mistake made when performing the undulating movement is an excessive movement up and down. As the movement originates from the head there is a tendency to over exaggerate this movement, causing the wave movement through the rest of the body to excessive and over pronounced. The swimmer then puts more effort and energy into moving up and down instead of actually swimming forwards.

A simple push and glide exercise from the poolside followed by a gentle undulating movement across the surface of the water help to eliminate any excessive body movements.

If the swimmer places the effort on using the undulation to move forward then this will provide a solid base from which to build and perfect butterfly stroke.

Leg Kick

The main functions of butterfly stroke leg action are to balance the arm action and help to provide some propulsion. This action then generates the undulating movement of the body position as the swimmer moves through the water.

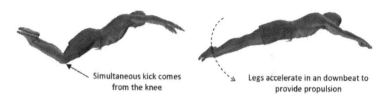

Simultaneous kick comes from the knee

Legs accelerate in an downbeat to provide propulsion

The legs kick simultaneously in an action that is similar to that of front crawl but with a greater and more pronounced knee bend.

The upbeat of the kick should come from the hip and the ankles should be relaxed with toes pointed. The legs move upwards without bending at the knees and the soles of the feet press against the water vertically and backwards.

Knees bend and then straighten on the downbeat to provide propulsion. The legs should accelerate to provide power on the downbeat.

Common leg kick mistakes

A breaststroke type leg kick can sometimes be performed by mistake, due to the simultaneous nature of the kick itself. Most swimmers that are able to perform breaststroke fairly well will naturally kick their legs in a small circle when attempting butterfly leg kick for the first time.

Another common mistake is to place an emphasis on the arm pull for butterfly and therefore lose all power from the leg kick. The legs just go through the motions when in fact they are needed to assist the body to rise out of the water so that the arm pull and recovery can be completed with minimum effort.

A powerful butterfly leg kick is vital and performing the kick whilst holding a float or kickboard out in front with straight arms will help develop the technique and power required for this movement.

Arms

Butterfly arm action is a continuous simultaneous movement that requires significant upper body strength. The action of the arms is similar to that of front crawl and the underwater catch, down sweep and upsweep parts draw the shape of a 'keyhole' through its movement path.

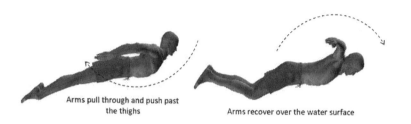

Arms pull through and push past the thighs

Arms recover over the water surface

Entry

The entry of the hands into the water should be fingertips first, leading with the thumb. Fingers should be together with palms flat and facing outwards. Arms should be stretched forward with a slightly bent elbow. Entry should be with arms extended inline with the shoulders.

Catch and down sweep

The pitch of the hands changes to a deeper angle with hands almost vertical. The catch and down sweep should begin just outside the shoulder line. Palms remain facing in the direction of travel. The elbow should bend to about 90 degrees to provide the extra power required. The hands sweep in a circular movement similar to breaststroke, but in a downward path.

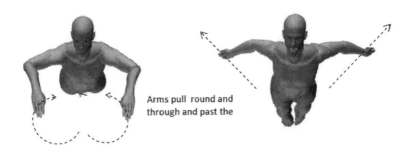

Arms pull round and
through and past the

Upsweep

The pitch of the hands changes to face out and upwards towards the water surface. Elbows extend fully to straighten the arms and hands towards the thighs.

Recovery

Hands and arms must clear the water on recovery in accordance with ASA Law. Arms and hands should exit the water little finger facing upwards. Arms must clear the surface as they are 'thrown' over and forwards. Palms remain facing outwards, naturally giving a thumb-first entry.

Common arm pull mistakes

The two most common mistakes made when it comes to butterfly arm technique are an incomplete or short pull and a wide hand entry.

The arm technique is sometimes compared to front crawl when it is taught to beginners in its most basic form. This is due to the long sweep and the recovery over the water surface. This is where the similarities end and this comparison can sometimes be taken literally, resulting in an almost double front crawl arm action with an excessive elbow bend.

The most common mistake made amongst slightly more advanced butterfly swimmers is a wide hand entry. The hands should enter the water inline with the shoulders. If the entry is wide of the shoulder line then this will result in a weak and inefficient arm pull.

Simply walking though shallow water of about shoulder depth practicing the arm action in slow motion will help to establish a full sweep and an inline hand entry.

Breathing

Breathing technique during butterfly is a rapid and explosive action.

Inhalation takes place as the arms complete their upsweep and begin to recover, as the body begins to rise. The head is lifted enough for the mouth to clear the water and the chin should be pushed forward, but remain at the water surface. Some exhalation underwater takes place during this phase.

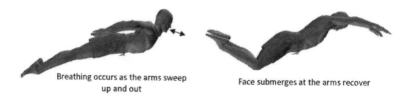

Breathing occurs as the arms sweep up and out

Face submerges at the arms recover

The head is lowered quickly into the water again as the arms recover inline with the shoulders, to resume an overall streamlined position and maintain minimal frontal resistance.

Explosive breathing is normally preferred but a combination of trickle and explosive breathing can be used. Explosive breathing involves a rapid exhalation followed immediately by inhalation, requiring powerful use of the respiratory muscles.

Common breathing mistakes

Failure to actually breathe is the most common mistake made by beginners learning butterfly breathing technique.

Because the inhalation and exhalation have to take place very quickly in the short second the face is being raised, it is very common to either inhale only or not breathe at all. The result: a pair of extremely inflated lungs and a severe lack of oxygen.

Performing the full stroke and taking a breath every other stroke cycle is a good way of ensuring that exhalation is taking place and that the lungs are sufficiently emptied before inhalation takes place.

Timing

The butterfly stroke cycle should contain 2 leg kicks to 1 arm cycle where the first kick occurs when the arms are forward and the second kick when the have pulled back.

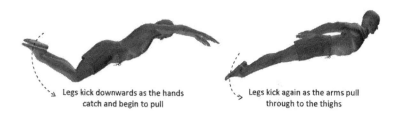

Legs kick downwards as the hands catch and begin to pull

Legs kick again as the arms pull through to the thighs

The downbeat of the first leg kick occurs at the catch and down sweep phase. Both arms will have been in the air during recovery, causing the hips to sink. The subsequent kick should be strong enough to counter balance this hip movement.

The second downbeat leg kick occurs during the powerful and accelerating upsweep phase of the arm cycle. During this movement, the feet react towards the hands and the strength will contribute towards propulsion.

Breathing can occur every stroke cycle or every other stroke cycle.

Common timing mistakes

Timing and coordination issues can occur when the swimmer attempts to kick and pull at the same time. There should be a delay from the leg kick as the arms pull, so that the first powerful leg kick assists the arms recovery.

Beginners learning butterfly tend to miss out the second supporting leg kick as the arms recover.

A good way to practice and develop the timing for this stroke is to swim using a butterfly leg kick and a breaststroke arm pull. There is less energy used when swimming with breaststroke arms because the arms recover under the water surface. Therefore it is an ideal way to ensure that there are two leg kicks for each arm pull, where one leg kick assists the body to rise and breathe, and the other smaller leg kick assists the arms to recover.

Once this exercise is perfected then the swimmer can reintroduce butterfly arms into the stroke and maintain the timing and coordination pattern.

Butterfly

exercises

BUTTERFLY: Body Position

Holding the poolside

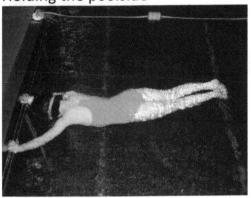

Aim: to practise the body position and movement by holding on to the poolside.

The swimmer performs an undulating action whilst using the poolside or rail for support. Note: this exercise should be performed slowly and without force or power as the static nature places pressure on the lower back.

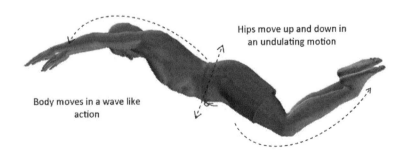

Hips move up and down in an undulating motion

Body moves in a wave like action

Key Actions

Keep your head in the middle
Make the top of your head lead first
Keep your shoulders level
Keep your hips level
Make your body into a long wave

Technical Focus

Exercise should be slow and gradual
Head remains central
Shoulders and hips should be level
Horizontal body with an undulating movement
Wave like movement from head to toe
Legs remain together

Common Faults

Body remains too stiff and rigid
Head moves to the sides
Shoulders and hips are not remaining level

BUTTERFLY: Body Position

Dolphin dives

Aim: to develop an undulating body movement whilst travelling through water of standing depth.

The swimmer performs a series of dives from a standing position, diving deep under the surface, arching the back and resurfacing immediately to stand up. The aim is to perform as many dolphin dives across the width as possible. Swimmers can then progress to performing the practice without standing in-between dives.

Body dives down and then resurfaces immediately in a wave like movement

Key Actions
Keep your head in the middle
Make the top of your head dive down first
Make your body into a huge wave
Stretch up to the surface

Technical Focus
Head remains central
Shoulders and hips should be level
Body moves with an undulating movement
Wave-like movement from head to toe
Legs remain together

Common Faults
Body remains too stiff and rigid
Body dives but fails to undulate upwards
Leading with the head looking forwards

BUTTERFLY: Body Position

Push and glide

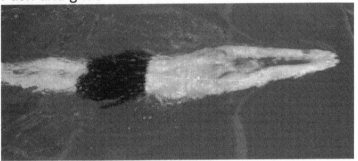

Aim: to practise and develop an undulating action whilst moving.

The swimmer pushes from the poolside into a glide and then begins the undulating action from head to toe. This allows the swimmer to experience the required undulating action whilst moving through the water.

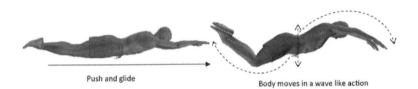

Push and glide

Body moves in a wave like action

Key Actions
Make the top of your head lead first
Keep your shoulders level
Keep your hips level
Make your body into a long wave
Pretend you are a dolphin swimming

Technical Focus
Head remains central
Shoulders and hips should be level
Body is horizontal with an undulating movement
Wave-like movement from head to toe
Legs remain together

Common Faults
Body remains too stiff and rigid
Shoulders and hips are not remaining level
Leading with the head looking forwards

BUTTERFLY: Legs

Sitting on the poolside

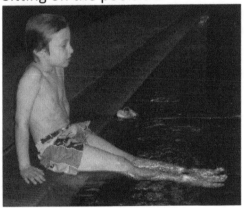

Aim: to develop the kicking action whilst sitting on the poolside.

Bending and kicking from the knees with legs together allows the swimmer to practise the correct movement and feel the water at the same time.

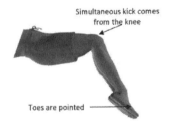

Simultaneous kick comes from the knee

Toes are pointed

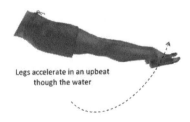

Legs accelerate in an upbeat though the water

Key Actions
Kick both legs at the same time
Keep your ankles loose
Keep your legs together
Point your toes

Technical Focus
Simultaneous legs action
Knees bend and kick in upbeat to provide propulsion
Legs accelerate on upbeat
Toes are pointed

Common Faults
Leg kick is not simultaneous
Toes are not pointed
Overall action is too stiff and rigid
Kick is not deep or powerful enough

BUTTERFLY: Legs

Push and glide adding leg kick

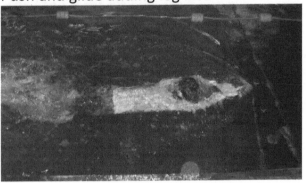

Aim: to practise the dolphin leg kick action and experience movement.

This allows the swimmer the develop propulsion from the accelerating leg kick and undulating body movement.

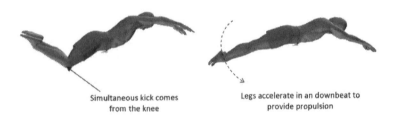

Simultaneous kick comes
from the knee

Legs accelerate in an downbeat to
provide propulsion

Key Actions
Keep your ankles loose
Kick downwards powerfully
Keep your legs together
Point your toes
Kick like a mermaid

Technical Focus
Simultaneous legs action
Knees bend and kick in downbeat to provide propulsion
Legs accelerate on downbeat
Toes are pointed
Hips initiate undulating movement

Common Faults
Leg kick is not simultaneous
Toes are not pointed
Overall action is too stiff and rigid
Kick is not deep or powerful enough

BUTTERFLY: Legs

Prone holding a float with both hands

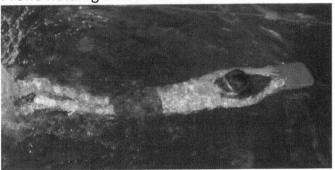

Aim: to develop the leg kick using a float for support.

This practice allows the advanced swimmer to develop leg kick strength and stamina as the float isolates the legs.

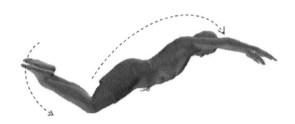

Powerful leg kick provides propulsion and help the body to undulate

Key Actions

Kick with both legs at the same time
Kick downwards powerfully
Keep your legs together
Create a wave-like action through your body
Kick like a mermaid

Technical Focus

Simultaneous legs action
Knees bend and kick in downbeat to provide propulsion
Legs accelerate on downbeat
Toes are pointed
Hips initiate undulating movement

Common Faults

Leg kick is not simultaneous
Toes are not pointed
Overall action is too stiff and rigid
Kick is not deep or powerful enough

BUTTERFLY: Legs

Supine position with arms by sides

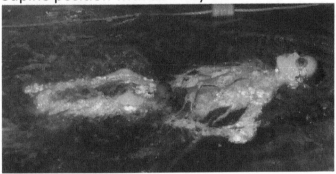

Aim: to practise and develop a dolphin leg kick action in a supine position.

This allows the swimmer to kick continuously whilst facing upwards. This practice requires a great deal of leg strength and stamina and therefore is ideal for developing these aspects of the stroke.

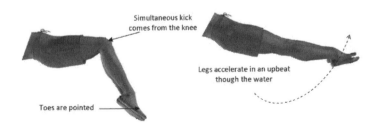

Simultaneous kick comes from the knee

Toes are pointed

Legs accelerate in an upbeat though the water

Key Actions

Kick both legs at the same time
Keep your ankles loose
Kick upwards powerfully
Keep your legs together
Point your toes

Technical Focus

Simultaneous legs action
Knees bend and kick in upbeat to provide propulsion
Legs accelerate on upbeat
Toes are pointed
Hips initiate undulating movement

Common Faults

Leg kick is not simultaneous
Overall action is too stiff and rigid
Hips are not undulating to initiate the kick
Kick is not deep or powerful enough

BUTTERFLY: Legs

Kick and roll

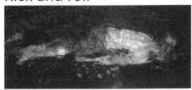 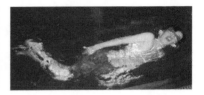

Aim: to combine the leg kick and undulating body movement and perform a rolling motion through the water.

This practice can be performed with arms held by the sides or held out in front. The rolling motion forces the swimmer to use the head, shoulders and hips to produce the movement required for powerful undulating propulsion.

Legs kick and body performs a 'cork screw' like roll through the water

Key Actions

Kick both legs at the same time
Keep your ankles loose
Roll like a corkscrew
Keep your legs together
Make your body snake through the water

Technical Focus

Simultaneous legs action
Head and shoulders initiate rolling motion
Knees bend and kick to provide propulsion
Legs accelerate on downbeat
Hips initiate undulating movement

Common Faults

Leg kick is not simultaneous
Overall action is too stiff and rigid
Kick is not powerful enough

BUTTERFLY: Arms

Standing on the poolside

Aim: to practise correct butterfly arm action whilst standing on the poolside.

The pupil is able to work through the arm action slowly and in stages so as to experience the basic movement required.

Arms pull through in a keyhole shape

Arms pull through and past the thighs

Key Actions

Move both arms at the same time
Thumbs go in first
Draw a keyhole under your body
Push past your thighs

Technical Focus

Arms move simultaneously
Hands enter the water in line with the shoulders
Hands pull in the shape of a keyhole
Hands push past the thigh

Common Faults

Arm action is not simultaneous
Arms are too straight
Arms are not pulling back to the thighs

BUTTERFLY: Arms

Walking on the pool floor

Aim: to progress from the previous practice and develop the arm action.

The swimmer can get a feel for the water whilst walking and performing the simultaneous arm action.

Arms pull through simultaneously

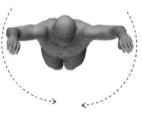

Arms are thrown forwards over the water surface

Key Actions

Move both arms at the same time
Thumbs go in first
Draw a keyhole under your body
Push past your thighs

Technical Focus

Arms move simultaneously
Hands enter the water in line with the shoulders
Hands pull in the shape of a keyhole
Hands push past the thigh

Common Faults

Arm action is not simultaneous
Arms are too straight
Fingers are apart
Hands fail to clear the water

BUTTERFLY: Arms

Push and glide adding arms

Aim: to practise the arm action whilst moving through the water.

Correct body position is established from the push and glide and the swimmer can then use the arm action to maintain momentum through the water. A limited number of arm pulls can be achieved with this practice.

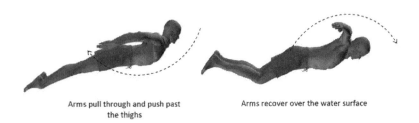

Arms pull through and push past
the thighs

Arms recover over the water surface

Key Actions

Move both arms at the same time
Thumbs enter water first
Pull hard through the water
Pull past your thighs
Throw your arms over the water

Technical Focus

Arms move simultaneously
Fingers closed together
Thumbs enter the water first
Hands enter the water in line with the shoulders
Hands push past the thigh
Hands clear water surface on recovery

Common Faults

Arms are too straight
Arms are not pulling back to the thighs
Hands fail to clear the water

BUTTERFLY: Arms

Arms only using a pull-buoy

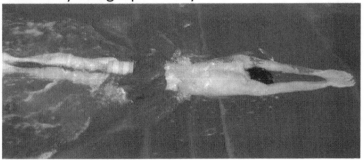

Aim: to help the swimmer develop arm strength and stamina.

This practice is performed over a longer distance, progressing from the previous practice. The pull buoy provides buoyancy and support as well as helps the undulating body movement.

Arms pull through the water with power

Hands and arms clear the water on recovery

Key Actions

Thumbs go in first
Pull hard through the water
Pull past your thighs
Throw your arms over the water

Technical Focus

Arms move simultaneously
Fingers closed together
Thumbs enter the water first
Hands enter the water in line with the shoulders
Hands push past the thigh
Hands clear water surface on recovery

Common Faults

Arms are too straight
Arms are not pulling back to the thighs
Hands fail to clear the water

BUTTERFLY: Arms

Arm action with breaststroke leg kicks

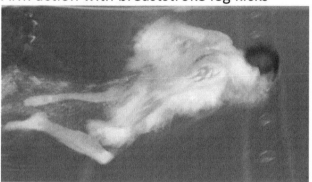

Aim: to enable use of breaststroke leg kicks to support the arm action.

As the legs kick, the propulsion helps the body to rise and the arms to recover over the water surface. This practice is also a good introduction to the timing of butterfly arms and legs.

Leg kick help the arms to recover over the water surface

Key Actions
Thumbs go in first
Draw a keyhole under your body
Pull past your thighs
Little finger comes out first
Throw your arms over the water

Technical Focus
Thumbs enter the water first
Hands pull in the shape of a keyhole
Hands push past the thigh
Little finger exits the water first
Hands clear water surface on recovery

Common Faults
Arms are too straight
Arms are not pulling back to the thighs
Fingers are apart
Hands fail to clear the water

BUTTERFLY: Breathing

Standing breathing, with arm pulls

Aim: to incorporate butterfly breathing into the arm action.

This practice is performed standing either on the poolside or stationary in water of standing depth.

Breathing occurs as the arms sweep up and out

Face submerges at the arms recover

Key Actions
Blow out hard as your chin rises
Put your face down as your arms recover
Push your chin forward and breathe every arm pull or every two
    arm pulls

Technical Focus
Breathing in should occur as the arms sweep up and out
Explosive breathing is most beneficial
Chin should remain in the water
Face dives into the water as the arms come level with the
    shoulders
Breath can be taken every stroke cycle or alternate cycles

Common Faults
Lifting the head too high
Arms stop recovery to breathe
Holding the breath

BUTTERFLY: Breathing

Full stroke

Aim: to use the full stroke to practice breathing, incorporating regular breaths into the arm and leg actions.

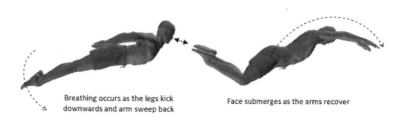

Breathing occurs as the legs kick downwards and arm sweep back

Face submerges as the arms recover

Key Actions

Blow out hard as your chin rises
Lift your head to breathe in as your legs kick down
Put your face down as your arms come over
Push your chin forward and breathe every arm pull or every two
arm pulls

Technical Focus

Breathing in occurs as the arms sweep upwards
Breathing in occurs as the legs are kicking downwards
Explosive breathing is most beneficial
Chin remains in the water
Face dives into the water as the arms come level with the
shoulders
Breath can be taken every stroke cycle or alternate cycles

Common Faults

Lifting the head too high
Arms stop recovery to breathe
Holding the breath
Breathing too often

BUTTERFLY: Timing

Full stroke

Aim: to perform the full stroke butterfly, incorporating two leg kicks per arm pull.

Legs kick downwards as the hands catch and begin to pull

Legs kick again as the arms pull through to the thighs

Key Actions
Kick hard as your hands enter the water
Kick again as your hands pull under your body

Technical Focus
Two legs kicks per arm cycle
Legs kick once as hands enter and sweep out
Legs kick once as arms sweep up and out

Common Faults
Only kicking once per arm cycle
Kicking too many times per arm cycle

"Now that you have finished my book, would you please consider writing a review? Reviews are the best way readers discover great new books. I would truly appreciate it."

Mark Young

For more information about learning to swim and improving your swimming strokes and swimming technique visit:

swim-teach.com

"The number one resource for learning to swim and improving swimming technique."

www.swim-teach.com